The Ro[...] Contract to Close

How to Successfully (and Easily) Manage the Details without Losing Your Mind – Or Your Clients

Wishing you Many Happy Closings –

Michelle Spalding

DEDICATION

To my three amazing children, Sean, Travis and Emily. You are an inspiration to me daily to live the very best life possible. Thank you for choosing me to be your Mom – I love you.

To Mom and Dad, thank you for encouraging me to just be me.

To Amy, Rhonda, and Penny. Each of you has had a profound impact in my life and without you I wouldn't be who I am today.

The Road from Contract to Close

CONTENTS

Introduction   x

1   The Big Picture   Pg 1

2   Making Money   Pg 9

3   Systems   Pg 15

4   Documents and Documentation   Pg 25

5   Communication   Pg 37

6   Documenting the Transaction   Pg 55

7   Managing the Details   Pg 67

8   Closing Day = Pay Day, Right?   Pg 73

9   Post-Closing & Fishing for Referrals   Pg 79

10 Effective Time Management   Pg 87

11 Working with a Virtual Assistant   Pg 93

12 Glossary and Terms   Pg 103

    Resources   Pg 123

ACKNOWLEDGMENTS

To Clurra Goodwin -Who helped me craft the perfect cover to bring this book to life. I'm thankful for your talent and friendship.

To Rhonda Ryder - The brilliant copywriter and amazing friend, thank you for helping me with the title and so many other things in life.

To Lorena Streeter - Thank you for helping me to edit my work into something that the public could actually read. You're a magician.

To Leann Graefe – Many of the lessons in this book were things we learned over the years of working together. Thank you for helping me to make TMC everything it is today and for sticking with me even during the craziest of times. You truly are an angel.

To the Team at TMC – I couldn't do it without you; thank you for choosing to be a part of TMC and the excellent work you do. Vesna Bodecker, Dawn Brooks, Diana Tria, Dayna Tobyansen, Beth Barnett and the many others who have helped make TMC what it is today.

To Carrie Gable & Angi Bell – Thank you for believing in me, the work I do and all your support over the years in this crazy business of real estate. Next bottle of wine is on me.

To the many wonderful clients of TMC - Thank you for allowing me to help you grow your business and sharing your passion for our services with your colleagues.

And finally.......

Thank you to YOU, the reader who wishes to better your skills and continue to raise your level of professionalism in the real estate industry. You humble me and encourage me to continue to do my part to make the home buying or selling experience better and better each day for everyone involved in the process.

<u>Special Notice</u>

While great care and research was undertaken to provide accurate and current information, the suggestions, comments, general principals, and conclusions contained in this publication are the opinions of the author and respective contributors.

The author, contributors, and publishers disclaim any responsibility for any liability, loss, or risk that may be claimed or incurred as a consequence, directly or indirectly.

References to any company or products and services do not constitute or imply endorsement or recommendation, and neither is any reference or absence of reference intended to harm, place a disadvantage, or in any other way affect any company or person. The author and contributors in many cases may have an interest in, be employed by, or consult for companies listed in this publication. Information contained in this publication should not be a substitute for common sense, thorough research, or competent advice.

Readers are urged to consult proper counsel or other authority regarding any points of law, finance, technology, and business before proceeding, and all conclusions expressed herein are subject to local, state, and federal laws or regulations.

Introduction

It's all about closing ...

No matter whether you are new to this fun business of real estate or have been at this for a while, there are always plenty of new things to learn, as the industry is constantly changing. That is probably why I've been so intrigued by real estate for so many years. For the last twenty years, I can honestly say that each day there has been something new to learn. The information in this book is based on my experience and that of the team I manage at Transaction Management Consultants, as well as the thousands and thousands of closings I've personally been a part of.

On the surface, the role of getting a transaction to close is really always the same, right? It's about ensuring that that the terms agreed upon in the contract are met, and that the deal funds. Certainly, some deals are easier than others. I've coordinated cash transactions that happened in just a few days, and worked on multiple gas station purchases that took over a year to get to closing. I once had a buyer go to jail the day before closing. Talk about a major letdown; we already had the loan docs at the title company and everything was ready to go. This was back in my days as a Realtor and my nice commission check disappeared along with the buyer.

You never truly know what is going to happen. In spite of those challenges and the many others I've had to face, I have also had the pleasure of working with many buyers and sellers to help them get to closing. In my career, I've received countless accolades for going the extra mile, and I've learned so much in the process. I know for a fact that most people want this process to be as smooth and painless as possible. I believe that by doing just a little extra, we're able to provide them with exactly that, and generally with much less work on our part. In

New Orleans, the little extra is called "lagniappe." I use that term with my team at TMC and I'm as thrilled as a pig in mud that they frequently receive totally unsolicited accolades from various parties in the transaction about their participation.

The residential real estate market is full of ups and downs for all the parties involved. Getting a buyer and seller to sign a contract is only the beginning of the process. While the job of managing a contract isn't usually glamorous, it's extremely important and, if done right, will result in more business from referrals than all your marketing dollars can generate. Think about how many times you've had a satisfying experience and told others. Likewise, how many times have you told someone how crummy an experience you had was? Now with Social Media the reach of the happy or unhappy customer can go that much further, and with lightning speed.

Keeping things moving forward smoothly will significantly improve the positive comments from those that you've done business with. It's not like we're talking about buying a shirt at the mall either; buying or selling a home is a pretty big experience and is **very, very** noticeable. Doing this part right will mean when someone asks the client you just worked with how it went, they will have nothing but **great** things to say.

Coordinating a transaction, from accepted contract throughout closing, is not like other business functions. Remember, *no one gets paid until something closes*. Your tasks will not occur in a linear fashion. It won't be coordinate an inspection, check that off, move on to coordinate the loan application, check that off, move on to track funding, check that off, etc.; you will be handling all of the tasks throughout, moving between tasks and issues as they arise. Additionally, the residential market is full of emotions, many which aren't of the happy variety. This can be magnified by sellers that are having financial problems and thus being forced to sell the property. It's important that you recall what you're there for, to help make the goal of closing happen. Sure it's stressful at times, but it's also extremely rewarding to know that you were part of such a historic event in the lives of the buyers and sellers.

While there's another book in itself to be written about all the great situations I've encountered, that's not the purpose of this material. Yes, you'll find a few stories in this book, my goal is to make sure that you understand the process, the role of everyone involved, some of the documents you'll encounter, and what to expect. It's also to help you find ways to make the entire process go smoother for all parties involved.

I am sure that soon you'll have your own stories to share, most of them good, about your real estate business. Keep in touch, and when that next book is written perhaps I'll be sharing one of your success stories.

Best wishes,

Michelle Spalding

"The man who makes no mistakes does not usually make anything." William Conner Magee

The Road from Contract to Close

"Long ago, I realized that success leaves clues, that people who produce outstanding results do specific things to create those results." Anthony Robbins

Chapter 1

YOUR BIG PICTURE

Before you can create a successful real estate business, you have to know what you want your business to provide you.

What inspired you to get into this business? Was it a friend or mentor who was successful? Was it an experience you'd had, that you felt if you were the one doing it, you could do it better? Was it the amount of money you thought you could make?

What do you want to achieve? Perhaps it's more money or flexibility. Maybe you want to open your own office or offices.

What dreams do you have for your business and life? For most, what they do is a means to get what they want. In other words, if you're selling homes, it's to generate an income that allows you to live the life you want. For others, it's to create a rental portfolio that provides them some security in their retirement. Both of those examples are about a life that you want, and real estate is the vehicle to get you there. Very few children want to grow up to be Realtors or real estate investors. What we all want is something bigger.

To reach our dreams, most of us find it helpful to create clear and concise goals. For our goals to be motivating and effective, however, they need to have a *why* within them, not be open-ended or vague. Generally, I find that people who aren't making the progress they would like, and are clearly capable of, aren't doing so because their goals aren't clearly defined. This is the step that trips most of us up.

Often we create resolutions around the New Year, and decide we want to lose weight (for example). Maybe we have a set number of pounds we expect to lose, a plan to do it by eating a certain way, and going to the gym frequently; however, without a real reason *why*, we likely won't be successful. Without the proper reflection within of why we want something, it's just a vague dream. It's generally not enough to convince us to make the big changes that are often necessary to fuel the transformation we want. Without a real motivating *why*, when it rains we won't be likely to go for a walk, or when chocolate cake shows up we'll find it hard to say no, even if we had a slice yesterday.

Let me further explain. Say your goal is to make more money. Maybe your *why* is that you want to pay off your debt; that's still vague, but if it's to pay off your debt and be an example to your children, that's better. The *why* is more compelling than simply stating that your goal is to make more money. This means when you're on your way to work and Starbucks is calling, you'll think about *why* you're only going there once a week rather than daily: the debt you're paying off, the promise you made to yourself and your family to accomplish this. It will become much easier to drive right by, especially if you have a photo of your kids on your dashboard!

Money, after all, is only paper or coins, it's not the money that we truly want when we set a goal like this, it's what the money can bring. We're not looking for a pile of cash because we want to have a pile of cash, we're looking for what we can do with it. In this example, pay off our debt and make our family proud.

No matter what your goals are, chances are they are something that, like many of us, you're always working on and thinking about, yet not quite reaching. Perhaps, like I found, it's because the *why* is not compelling enough. With a clear, defined *why*, the *how* you'll accomplish them becomes easy. People, resources, and opportunities appear out of places we didn't expect or see before.

Not too long ago I met with a new agent who desired to close twenty transactions in his first year. He had that number in his mind, but no reason why. He'd come to me for help in coordinating his transactions. He knew his strength was in working with buyers and sellers, not in coordinating and keeping up with the documentation; smart guy! Anyway, as we chatted he told me about his goal to sell twenty houses. I congratulated him and asked him where that number came from and why he wanted to sell twenty. He paused for a while, and then said "I guess that's what I think I can do." I offered to coach him a bit and asked him some probing questions to help find out if twenty was really the number, and what his *why* was. Here are some of the questions I asked him:

- ☐ What do you want your real estate business to provide you?

- ☐ Why do you want this? What do you plan to do with this?

- ☐ How much will it cost you, in money and time, to get this?

- ☐ Are you willing to pay this?

- ☐ What happens if you don't reach your goal?

As he went through this exercise with me, he got really clear on what he wanted. He had been in a job before where he'd given his company 100 percent. Sadly, his company fell on hard times and he was laid off and never called back into work. Being out of work had taken a toll on his savings, and he thought by selling twenty houses he would be able to meet his monthly responsibilities and have some left to begin to replenish his savings. On the surface this sounds pretty good, but not compelling enough to do what it takes to sell twenty houses your first year. The more he thought about it and got really clear about what he wanted, he found his *why*. He wanted to be able to give 100 percent and receive that and then some in return for his investment into a company; *his* company in this case. In the end, he realized that he no longer wanted to rely on anyone else for his financial needs. After we looked at this goal of twenty together, he realized that this *why* was to create his own future, and to no longer rely on others.

It would be hard for him if his only goal was twenty transactions. He'd already figured out that his income didn't require twenty. However, after he and I spoke and did a coaching session together, he realized that he really wanted security and to be appreciated by those he worked for. Knowing his *why* helped him when things got a little hairy throughout the year. It helped motivate and inspire him to keep moving forward; at the end of the year, he had exceeded his original goal. His *why* helped him by taking the pressure off meeting a transaction number and to just stay connected to the reason he got into this business.

With a clear understanding of exactly what you want, why you want it, and how it's done, you'll find that it's easier than you thought it could be; your focus is on doing whatever needs to be done to reach your goal instead of fretting over how you're going to get there, and doubting your ability.

Too often we have a tendency to say that we want more; we get excited about it, then the excitement changes to an overwhelming feeling once we get started and face a challenge or unexpected twist in the road. When we have a clear *why*, our focus is on that, not the challenge, and therefore the solutions come to us faster and easier.

The goal for the information you're reading in this book is to help you achieve success in getting your real estate transactions closed—smoothly, successfully, and with the least amount of hassle on your part. With the right focus on *why* you want to build your real estate business, the right amount of *how* to get the deals you've put together closed from this book, you'll have more time and energy to devote to the things that you're really passionate about.

Before I share with you some of the strategies and stories of getting transactions closed, I want to encourage you to take some time and discover what you really want out of your real estate business. Like the example above, it's not to close twenty transactions, it's so that you could have the satisfaction in knowing you are in control of your income and future.

Having a real estate business can provide many freedoms and opportunities. Some of my favorites are:

☐ **Family** – creating a legacy for your children is so important. Teaching them the importance of balancing family and business or career is only done by example. Being able to check out, go on school field trips, days at the beach, or just being there when they come home from school is truly what you want to be remembered for.

☐ **Financial** - the ways to make money in real estate are almost endless. When you trade your time for money, that's called a J.O.B. When you have a business, your income is truly only limited by you. *How powerful!*

☐ **Independence –** being in charge of your future, your finances, and your time is just a part of the independence you have as a real estate entrepreneur. If you're like me, having a real boss doesn't excite you; I chose to be the boss – for the most part I like who I work for, and I'm sure you will, too.

☐ **Freedom –** Having the opportunities to do the things

you want, when you want, affords you the ability to do the things that make you happy. For many, myself included, traveling is freedom. Maybe freedom for you is the ability to take off an afternoon to spend time enjoying your favorite hobby, or a movie.

No matter what you desire in life, all things are possible once you know what they are.

There are as many reasons for having your own real estate business as there are real estate entrepreneurs. Each of us starts a business for our own unique reason(s). The above are just some of the top ones I've discussed with others. Think about why you're in this, what you want and don't want. The answers may not come today, but with some serious thought you'll find your *why*, which will help you reach the goals you set for yourself.

- ☐ So what inspires you?

- ☐ Why did you decide to make real estate your business?

- ☐ What do you want your real estate business to provide you?

- ☐ Why do you want this? What do you plan to do with this?

- ☐ How much will it cost you, in money and time, to get this?

- ☐ Are you willing to pay this?

- ☐ What happens if you don't reach your goal?

- ☐ I encourage you to stop for a moment, right now, and jot down why you decided to start your own real estate business. Then keep the page you create handy, post it on the wall in your office where it's in clear sight, and look at it often. You may even want to make copies of it and hang it in other places where you'll regularly be reminded of why you are doing this, especially when things aren't going exactly the way you'd like them to.

My reason for starting a real estate business is:

_____

_____

_____

_____

_____

_____

_____

Now that you've identified clearly why *you* are in this business, I hope that you do everything possible to have more of what you want. Whatever brings you joy should be your number one priority every day. The more you focus on what you really want, what really drives you, the easier it will be to achieve the success you desire for yourself.

Set aside a regular time each day to review your reason(s) for having a real estate investing business. Maintaining your focus is critical in achieving success. Keep a copy of this brief paragraph you create in your journal, or your calendar, and post where you'll see it throughout the day.

 Bright Idea - Keep an eye on your goals, keep an eye on your time, and limit distractions. Don't wait until December to see what you've done or haven't; review them frequently, adjust where needed, and accomplish what you really desire to do.

"Success seems to be connected with action.
Successful people keep moving.
They make mistakes, but they don't quit."
Conrad Hilton

"I definitely wanted to earn my freedom. But the primary motivation wasn't making money, but making an impact." Sean Parker

Chapter 2

MAKING MONEY

In the real estate industry there is a lot of time and attention paid to the many experts on sales and marketing. Yes, those are essential to creating customers, yet they are only part of the pie. As said before, getting a transaction closed is where the payday occurs and therefore it's critical to stay on top of it.

Now before I go too far here, and you put this book down thinking that "she is just another one of those greedy people, or only thinking about the money" let me stop for a moment and address that.

Business is about making money; there is absolutely nothing to be ashamed about if you want to make lots of it.

You can make money without hurting or taking from others. That is the way I run my business and coach clients to do so. I know that the more income I create, the more good things I can do. Not just vacations, but trips to places where I can help, where I can volunteer my time *and* my resources to make a difference in the lives of others. To places where people who weren't as fortunate as myself have been born in. With money, I can donate to charitable organizations that have programs to help others. I can pay for a quality education for my children and grandchildren... you get the picture; it's more than just fancy cars, nice houses or designer goods, none of which are bad, but they are not everything either.

I once heard someone explain it this way: being sick along with someone doesn't help them heal faster. So how can being broke or financially challenged bring you any closer to helping others? It can't! No one will benefit by you being broke, absolutely no one.

You're right, we can give of our time, but if we can't pay our bills because we're not running our business successfully, then how much time do we have to offer someone else?

Over the years many Realtors I've met, and even others alike start businesses, but don't treat what they do as a business. They've come from a J.O.B., into selling homes and treat it like a J.O.B. They wait for people to come to them, rather than seeking them out. They sit by and complain rather than look for solutions. While they may "claim" to be business owners, they aren't entrepreneurs.

Entrepreneurs, are different; they look for ways to create the business they want, they understand the *why*. They are doing what they want.

Entrepreneurs get that there are twenty-four hours in a day, and that we all have the same time. Successful enterprising entrepreneurs, in real estate or any other business realize that what will allow them to create the income and life they desire is the way they use their time.

It takes a certain mindset to be a successful entrepreneur; one who has the financial resources to do the things that are important to them, as well as the things that they *want* to do.

Recently I was having lunch with a real estate coach who used our transaction coordinating services prior to changing her business and now exclusively coaching agents. We're both into mindset, personal and professional growth, and frequently spend a lot of the time we have together discussing some of the new ideas and action steps we've learned. At this particular lunch the topic was around money and how having a lack mentality is a huge block she sees in the agents she works with.

As we further discussed it I told her I'd discovered the same here when people call to get info on what our transaction coordinators do and the costs associated with it.

In some calls people balk at the cost, telling me that they've had someone in the past who'd done the work for much less. Often when I ask them why they are looking for someone new I hear one of two things, first one – they aren't happy with the quality of the work he/she is performing. The second one – that person is no longer in business. At other times I get calls and when I share the costs they say, "Wow, that's all?" To which I always remind them that tips and bonuses are always appreciated. People in the same line of work, looking for solutions to their challenges, and some see the cost as an obstacle, while others see it as a way to achieve a goal they have for themselves.

Over the years I've learned that while we may have a conscious belief that we can and should make a certain amount of money, it's a subconscious belief that often stops us from achieving what we really desire. While this may seem like a challenge to some, it's really an opportunity to make a change that will allow us to have what we want.

For instance, most of us grew up with some ideas about money that were given to us by our parents, grand-parents or other influential adults in our lives. Many of us have heard all the same things such as "money doesn't grow on trees," "money is the root of all evil," "that's too expensive," or "only the rich get richer and the poor get poorer." While we may not want to believe these statements, they are such a part of our core belief system that the only way to move past them and the limiting beliefs they have in our lives is to change their meaning to us.

Not long ago I did this exercise and here's the way I changed a few of them:

- ☐ *Money doesn't grow on trees...but it does come from the ideas that grow within me and that allow me to help others and create a better world through my services.*

- ☐ *Money is the root of all evil...when used by people for evil. I am a good person with a big heart and use my prosperity for greatness.*

- ☐ *That's too expensive is an old idea I no longer believe. This is an investment in my joy.*

- ☐ *Only the rich get richer and the poor get poorer...maybe in your reality, but in mine there is an unlimited source of abundance and it's mine for the asking.*

Just a few tweaks to the way I looked at the statements I'd heard for most of my life transformed the way I looked at money and prosperity. Give this little exercise a try; think about the things you heard growing up that come up when you think about money and give them a new meaning. I've added mine to Evernote so that I can reference them anytime I need a little reminder, as well as add to them when I notice another limiting belief.

As our lunch continued, my coach friend said "the problem is that most agents are too cheap: they expect people to invest in them, to do business with them, and to pay the fees they want but they aren't willing to invest with others." While this may work when they are starting out, she knows firsthand from her years in business that they will never achieve long term success if they aren't willing to make an investment in growing their business with something like leveraging their time by using a transaction coordinator or hiring a part-time assistant to help them with their marketing.

Sure, shifting our mindset about money takes effort yet is so, so simple at the same time. Perhaps it's the simplicity that stumps us initially, expecting that to make more money we have to work harder when in the end the truth is all we have to do is work smarter.

No matter what you do in life, whether it's as a Realtor, a real estate investor, a transaction coordinator, or any other chosen business, without the mindset of prosperity you will always struggle to make the money you so rightfully deserve.

"The difference between great people and everyone else is that great people create their lives actively, while everyone else is created by their lives, passively waiting to see where life takes them next. The difference between the two is the difference between living fully and just existing." Michael Gerber

Chapter 3

CREATING SYSTEMS FOR YOUR BUSINESS

Many years ago I read the book *The E-myth Revisited* by Michael Gerber. I can say without a shadow of doubt that it's been one of the most influential books in my business and has transformed the way I look at things. Initially, when I read it, I was a sales agent and thought, that's nice, Mr. Gerber, but how will this apply to me? And with some creativity, the help of a coach, and being willing to see things differently, I began to envision a real estate business where I wasn't the one doing everything.

Each year I pick up my tattered copy and read it again, and I always get a new idea and a fresh bit of inspiration which I can use to help me with my business. The core idea in the book is to create systems that allow you to go from the worn out, exhausted person who does it all in a business, to the entrepreneur who leads the business and the people involved in it.

Systems are the foundation for the success of your real estate business, especially from contract to close. Without a map or a way to effectively manage your deals, you will spend too much time on the phone chasing things, and not enough time making new deals.

Sometimes when I ask real estate agents if they have a task list they follow once they have a transaction under contract, they confess that they don't. One person told me that her method was to say a prayer and do whatever she needed to as it became necessary. This way of thinking and managing the contract limits the amount of time you have as well as mental energy to do other things.

Often when I'm speaking at an office or an event, and I meet with new agents, they tell me they are so excited as they start out with their first deal, and they want to make sure that nothing goes wrong. They want to learn how to do this process before they delegate it to someone else. Some tell me it's almost fun to call and check with the other parties on the status of the deal: Where the lender is with financing approval, where the title company is with clearing any title issues, etc. After a while, they learn that the time spent making those calls detracts from the core of their business, which is finding more people to work with and getting them under contract.

One of the team leaders at an office meeting I was speaking at once said "no more money is made on the deal after the contract is signed." Meaning no matter whether you're calling for an update or your transaction coordinator is, you're not going to make more money on this deal. You've got to constantly be working on putting new ones together.

If you don't have a checklist or a system you follow, you can pick up a copy of a comprehensive checklist I created that will guide you through almost any real estate transaction. These are exactly what we use at Transaction Management Consultants to keep on top of thousands and thousands of transactions each year. In chapter 6 of this book I go over the checklist my team uses.

Checklists are designed to help you take what you need to do out of your head and to put them into an effective management system to track and oversee. They also will help you immensely if you are working with a business partner, or have hired or are planning to hire someone to assist you in this process.

Still not convinced that you need checklists? Read on...

Medical checklists

Renowned John Hopkins Hospital critical-care specialist Dr. Peter Pronovost put together a simple five-step checklist in 2001 for installing lines in the human body during care. Almost immediately, infection rates plummeted at John Hopkins. He shared the results and the checklist with a handful of the worst hospitals in the country and within the first three months of the program in Michigan the infection rate of Michigan ICUs decreased by sixty-five percent.

Checklists inspired by the B-17 bomber

Boeing almost went bankrupt when one of their top pilots crashed a newly-designed bomber right in front of top military brass. Realizing their new generation of aircraft was *too complicated for even the best pilots*, Boeing created a simple checklist and proceeded to sell over 13,000 planes that flew over 1.8 million miles without a crash.

Brilliant, highly educated people use them every day to make sure they don't miss an important step. Now it's your turn. Time to download what's in your head and create some checklists to streamline your real estate business.

Systems are the core of any successful business. Without knowing daily what activities should be done to create income, you find yourself doing busy things and then at the end of the day never get to the big things because there just isn't enough time. How many times have you thought about doing something, even written it on a to-do-list, yet never got to it?

While there are many reasons for that, the number one is generally that you didn't have a system for getting things done.

Systems are an essential part of any business and real estate is no exception. However, for far too long real estate was glamorized by many as a business you could do all alone. One that all you had to do was put a property under contract to make money.

While that is true to some extent, it's really only a scratch in the surface of what it really takes to be successful in this business. As I often say when speaking, "*no one gets paid until something closes.*" Therefore, getting deals closed is where the payoff occurs, and you darn well better have a way in place to ensure what needs to happen, actually does.

For a very long time I've been talking about systems. It's been a passion of mine since reading and implementing *The E-myth Revisited* many years ago. For me and many others, it is the best instruction on being an entrepreneur out there. I'll do my best to touch on it here in this chapter; however, I highly recommend that you also pick up a copy yourself. This is required reading for each client I coach. It's one of those books that once you've read it, you'll find that a refresher is helpful. It's like taking a bath; once isn't enough.

In 2008, I had the privilege of meeting Mr. Gerber at an event in Orlando. Earlier that year we were both a part of a real estate training course online, which was part of Real Estate Radio USA.

Yes, I can officially say I shared the same virtual stage as my hero Michael Gerber.

For the record, a system is "any formulated, regular, or special method or plan of procedure" according to Dictionary.com.

A system is what you or someone else has created as a way to get things done each and every time. However, systems are constantly evolving, as we learn and grow, and as our businesses do, as well.

Remember that what you're creating is a real estate business, not a J.O.B. A *job* requires you to be there to make money, where a business is something that you can grow through leverage to allow you to create more income with less time. A business can give you *freedom* when you create systems in it and bring in people to help you implement those systems.

The first time I read *The E-Myth Revisited*, I was in real estate sales. I'd never heard of the idea of systemizing the steps necessary to run a business. While the idea of having someone help me was very appealing, I wasn't sure I could do it. Like everyone else I've met over the years, I was fearful of change, worried that if I took a chance on someone, they might mess things up. Or that they would be really good and steal my business model and the clients I worked with.

I didn't realize that I had to, in order to increase my revenue and to have a life. After reading this book, my entire practice changed dramatically for the better. I learned there were so many things I was doing that I wasn't the most qualified for, and there were many things I needed to be doing that I wasn't making the time for. Putting stamps on postcards, which I thought initially was important because it was how I generated business, wasn't really what an entrepreneur should be doing. Those were activities I should have outsourced or paid one of my children to do for me. Likewise, I had little time I spent brainstorming, creating, and working "on" my business not "in" it.

Looking back, I see why Mr. Gerber tells us that so many businesses fail. I clearly "felt" it and saw that there was a ceiling in my business that I would get to, and I would either have to get help, or stop at that level and accept that it was as far as I was going to be able to go.

Settling is not something I'm comfortable accepting, so I

decided to make some changes to ready myself for the business I truly sought, one that would give me the freedom that I desired.

How did I start creating systems for my business, you may ask? Simple: one step at a time. First, I started documenting everything I did on a regular basis. I felt that it would be difficult to train someone and work at the same time. I also realized that some people you invest time in to train just don't work out. I needed a manual, a system to run my business. I also needed a vacation and was in no position at that point to take one, as my entire business required me to do it all.

To change things, I took a few hours over a few weeks and wrote down everything I did on a regular basis, things like check e-mail, reply to buyer and seller inquires, lead follow-up, closing procedures, listing procedures, etc.

After I had my list created, I set out to document written instructions for every aspect of it. Over the course of a few months, I created a very detailed description of how my unique real estate business ran. Scripts for buyer and seller inquires, email templates for consistent replies, and instructions for my listing and closing actions. This turned out to be quite an undertaking, but one that I was proud I'd accomplished. After I was done I shared it with the broker I was working with and we turned portions of it into an office manual for the firm. When a new agent joined her organization, she was able to simply review the system with them, and provide them with reference book to use for managing their own successful real estate business. It's just up to them to follow the guide and make it happen.

Finding strength and power in this exercise was a real eye opener. I learned that many of the things that I thought were important to the day to day flow of my business really didn't need to be done by me. As a matter of fact, there were others who were better at it, and slowly I changed the way I handled my business.

With documented systems, you have the ability to really look at the way you're running your business. Also, you have the ability to quickly and easily bring people in to help you grow your business. You'll find that the person you hire is far more successful when they know exactly what you expect of them, and have easy to follow instructions that explain what steps they need to take to fulfill their job.

Have you ever had one of those jobs where you were given verbal instructions, told to take notes and trained at 100 miles an hour, think you have it down, only to be hauled into the boss's office to be told 'NOT!'? Then you'll appreciate how empowering having written systems are in the success of your employee(s).

Each business is unique, and requires systems from the training you've received, books you've read, and information you've learned from others. That blend makes it yours and yours alone. Taking action to systems to run your business and work smarter is the first step in achieving the results you want.

*****

I love to teach on this subject, and often when I do workshops and start chatting with people about systems they tell me they are creative, or don't like following rigid rules. Okay, so I bite, and rather than challenge their statement, I like to get them to see the necessity within themselves.

I ask them about what they want their business to look like and do for them, and generally it's many of the things that I mentioned in the previous chapter; more time with family, flexibility, freedom, financial gains, etc. I then ask them about their marketing, what they're doing, how it's working, and generally we find that they've discovered something that makes the phone ring. I ask them to identify the number of hours they are spending "doing" their thing. Pretty soon, they realize that without some rules, or some system, they will not only be the only one doing everything, but they will not have the things they wanted from their business. It's great to see their faces change, for them to have this 'ah ha' moment, like a light bulb has gone on and they now can see the craziness in their thinking. When I work with coaching clients individually, the next step is to have them really get clear about what they want, what they don't want, and work together to find ways to make it happen.

***

In a real estate business, with very few exceptions, the payday occurs when a transaction closes. Because this is such a critical part of the business, it's one that I'm very passionate about. It's not the sexy part, it's the grunge part, where the rubber meets the road and sometimes it rears its ugly side. I liken it to giving birth. Having done that a few times, I'm pretty familiar with what happens. It's simply something we go through to get the baby.

Going through the process from contract to close isn't something that someone wakes up one day and says, "hey, Hon, remember that fun we had last year when we sold our house, all the drama, the twists, and the crazy people we met along the way? Let's get a deal under contract so we can go through that again!" No, they only do it because they want to buy or sell a home.

So when we're in the phase of contract to close, the pressure is on to make sure that all the "i's" are dotted, the "t's" are crossed, and that things go as quickly and smoothly as possible. Unfortunately, there are many times where you're dealing with people who aren't as professional as you, or as much as you'd like them to be. Since you're only as strong as your weakest link, the link that's not doing his or her part of their job in helping get this transaction closed has to be helped by someone else, whether we like it or not.

When a lender doesn't return your calls, or a surveyor doesn't go out to the property the day scheduled, you can't stop and blame them, or throw a fit and sit by and wait. However, I have seen this happen on many occasions. I believe when things don't go our way, we have to do, as I tell my daughter, is "put on your big girl shoes and go kick some butt."

In other words, "you've got to take action!" You're going to have to do things that are "outside" of what your role generally is. This is where knowing exactly what needs to happen and keeping on top of it is critical to the success of this transaction and the future of your business.

Over the years in helping Realtors and real estate investors create fulfilling and profitable businesses, I've discovered that *most* have no system for managing their transactions. They simply get it under contract and start praying, nagging, and hoping that it will close and they receive their hard-earned commission.

There are others I meet who have checklists that they simply don't use, or start and forget to maintain. Without systems in place, it's nearly impossible for you to have anyone other than *you* do the work needed to run your real estate business.

It's your life, it's your business, it's up to you to decide how you want to live it, and then make it happen.

"The ability to concentrate and to use your time well is everything if you want to succeed in business—or almost anywhere else for that matter." Lee Iacocca

Chapter 4

DOCUMENTS AND DOCUMENT REVIEW

No matter where you live or what part of the country you practice real estate in, it's no secret that real estate transactions involve an overwhelming amount of paperwork. There are disclosures, contracts, addenda, inspection reports, loan information, and title information, just to name a few. I've got clients in California and we joke that there are disclosures for the disclosures and an addendum to the addendum and disclosures for each addendum and… Well, you get the picture. There is a lot of paper being used just to get a home under contract on the West Coast.

Thankfully, we now have the ability to sign documents electronically and manage the entire process from contract to close without much, if any, paper. Should you choose to handle transactions by paper, be prepared for lots of it. Going digital is easy and avoids the need for piles of paper. It also allows you to take your business anywhere, which, for me, someone who *loves* to travel, means I can do what I need to from here or any other place in the world.

I highly suggest you dump the paper and utilize some form of an online platform to manage your transactions. Going digital also allows you to access or share this information at the click of a mouse via the Internet.

Without a doubt, any document that you are completing or reviewing as part of your transaction should be examined closely. If there is an initial missing, a date, or anything, basically, this could cause a delay in closing or worse, give someone a way out of the contract. Making sure that all the "i's" are dotted and the "t's" are crossed in the beginning of the contract will help eliminate unnecessary and painful headaches later on down the road.

One of my pet peeves is contract dates and it's one that is confusing for those involved, especially your buyer or seller. *Please* when you're writing, or helping prepare any document that relates to when a closing date is to take place, pick up a calendar and check to see what day of the week the date you're thinking about falls on. More often than I can count I've seen contracts with closing dates of Saturday, Sunday, or a bank holiday.

All of these are days where closings generally do not take place, so this means that when a contract is received with a date that falls on one of these three, it has to be discussed with everyone and later agreed that we really meant Monday, not Sunday. The thirty seconds it would have taken to look at the calendar will potentially save loads of time in the future.

Before I go into the documents, I want to share with you the importance of using the correct documents. When I worked at the law firm many years ago, we had a client come in one day who was delighted that he'd finally secured a buyer for his business. He had negotiated the terms with the buyer and then written it up on the standard real estate contract that is used in Florida, called the FAR/BAR. Okay, you might be thinking... "so what's wrong with this?"

Well, the problem was, he wasn't selling any real estate, he was selling a business. There were so many things he'd agreed to in the contract and many things that were left out. After meeting with the attorney it was agreed that a new contract specific to the sale of the business was necessary. After the seller met with the buyer to discuss the need for a new document, the buyer had a change of heart about the price. The seller ended up accepting $8,000 less than the originally agreed upon amount when the buyer signed the new and accurate contract. The buyer had him, as we say, "over a barrel." Sure he could have waited, but he chose not to, and the mistake of using the wrong contract cost him.

Here is a list of the documents we'll cover in this section:

- ☐ Sales Contract
- ☐ Addendum(s)
- ☐ Disclosures
- ☐ Receipt for Deposit
- ☐ Buyer financing pre-approval letter
- ☐ Buyer financing loan commitment or approval
- ☐ Inspection Report
- ☐ Appraisal
- ☐ Title Commitment
- ☐ Loan Application
- ☐ Note
- ☐ Mortgage
- ☐ Truth In Lending Disclosure also called TIL
- ☐ Amortization Schedule
- ☐ Lien
- ☐ Warranty Deed

Some of these items only get a small paragraph as they are not documents you'll be completing, only reviewing. Others, such as the sale contract, have several pages of details.

Sales Contract - Each state uses slightly different contracts, but they're all similar. The sales contract is simply an agreement between a buyer and seller to convey the property at an agreed upon price with agreed upon terms. The sales contract spells out the specifics and the timeline and is a legally binding document.

Listed below are the most common elements of a sales contract:

The sales contract in most states is a form that is simply filled in and can be adjusted based on the terms to the specific transaction. There may be boxes to check who is paying for what, as well as blanks to complete with specific dates or dollar amounts. *Some states require that contracts be prepared by an attorney, therefore this section may not apply.*

There are several key elements found in almost all contracts outlined as follows:

☐ **Names of parties** – This section addresses who is purchasing the property and who the seller is. It's very important to confirm the correct spelling if you are completing this form.

☐ **Property description** – This section describes the property by street address and generally provides the legal description as well.

☐ **Personal property** – Many contracts now have the most commonly left personal property items pre written. There is also a space to include other items and generally a space to omit items.

☐ **Figures** – The sales price, escrow deposit, additional deposit, home warranty, seller contribution to closing costs, and anticipated loan amount, etc. are all part of the contract.

☐ **Terms** – If the buyer is applying for financing, this section will outline the terms the buyer is willing to accept to purchase this property. This section also provides the agreed upon deadline for the buyer to apply for financing and for the buyer to provide the loan commitment. These dates are critical to the transaction and must be monitored. If this is an owner-financed transaction, those terms are detailed here.

☐ **Title charges** – This will determine who will pay for the title charges, such as the owner's title policy. Generally, whoever is paying for the owner's title policy is who selects the title agent.

☐ **Closing date** – This section outlines the date that closing will take place. It is often written as "on or before" and then the date.

☐ **Inspections** – The agreed upon time for the buyer to inspect the property and report findings to the seller. There may be a different section for the WDO or termite inspections. These trigger dates are critical to the transaction and must be monitored.

☐ **Home Warranty** – Many contracts have a section that outlines who will pay for the home inspection, if applicable, and what amount the party will pay. It generally indicates the agreed upon company that the warranty will be provided by.

☐ **Addendum** – If there are addenda, there should be a check box or list in the sales contract to reflect the addendum attached to the contract. This prevents misunderstandings in the future and ensures that everyone knows what addenda are parts of this contract.

☐ **Special remarks or clauses** – Sometimes you will find this section where the buyer and seller have agreed upon certain terms, such as the seller contributing to closing costs of the buyer. In addition, if there are special terms such as lease back, early occupancy, or what have you, you may find them here in the special remarks or clauses section.

☐ **Brokerage commission amounts** – If applicable, this will state the commission amounts.

☐ **Signatures** – This is where the parties will sign, agreeing to the terms. The dates are critical as well, as the "clock" starts when the last person signs.

☐ **Effective date** – Some contracts now call for an agreed upon effective date. This eliminates confusion in deadlines as it's easy to calculate from this agreed upon *written* date.

Assignment of Contract:

The Assignment of Contract is used in transactions where the buyer named in the contract is now assigning his interest to another person, generally for a fee. The end buyer is now who will close on the transaction. *Note: make sure the sales contract you are using allows for this. One of the most important items in the assignment is the assignment fee. This lets the title company know the amount the buyer has agreed to pay you at the time of closing.*

Common Addendum and Disclosures:

There are endless addenda and disclosures; it's impossible to review them all in this book. By the time it would get to you, it's possible and probable that new ones would be created. Additionally, each state has slightly different requirements. There are some that are more popular and those I've chosen to review here.

☐ **Home Owner's Association (HOA) Disclosure** – In communities where there is an HOA, this disclosure is provided by the seller to let the buyer know of the fees, and often the amenities.

☐   **Condo Disclosure** – The condo disclosure is very similar to the HOA disclosure; it's designed to let the buyer know what fees and amenities are in this condo.

☐   **Lead-Based Paint Disclosure** – Homes built prior to 1978 may have lead-based paint in the home. This disclosure is to alert the buyer of this possibility and their signature on the disclosure generally acknowledges receipt of information relating to lead-based paint.

☐   **Seller's Disclosure** – This form is generally completed by the seller and provided to the buyer "disclosing" any known material defects of the property. Generally this disclosure is used in transactions where there are Realtors involved.

☐   **Mold Disclosure** - Completed by the seller to disclose to the buyer if they are aware of any mold issues with the house and if so, what has been done. It is acknowledged by the buyer as a part of the contract.

<u>Receipt for Deposit</u> - The receipt for deposit is critical for determining that the buyer or their agent has actually delivered the deposit. I've seen in the past where a copy of the escrow deposit made payable to *"So and So Title"* was never delivered and therefore the funds never cleared the buyer's bank.

Later the buyer defaults or fails to perform as agreed upon in the contract. What does he/she care? They have no earnest money on the line, no "skin in the game." Sadly, the seller has no knowledge of this and thinks he has recourse to make a claim for the deposit.

Later it's discovered that the slimy or lazy agent on the buyer's side simply says "It got lost in the mail." If the escrow deposit was never delivered then the seller will likely never see any portion of his/her claim for this deposit.

In many states it is now required by the real estate licensing board that a receipt for deposit be received and kept in the file. Long before it became a law, my coordinating company always obtained a receipt from the entity holding the deposit so that there were no unpleasant surprises.

Buyer financing pre-approval letter – Pre-approval letters vary from lender to lender. The important thing to note on all of them to confirm that they are actually worth something is the language that indicates the buyer's credit has been pulled, and a preliminary determination has been made based upon that, and other criteria that the buyer is "pre-approved."

It's my opinion, and that of others, that a "pre-qualification" letter is only about as good as the forms we all receive in the mail soliciting us for new credit cards. It says, sure we'd like to give you a loan (or a credit card), but until you complete this form and let us look at your credit we won't make any commitment to do anything.

It's extremely important to know the difference between a pre-qualification and a pre-approval letter, if you're not sure ASK A LENDER to explain. Most will be happy to do so.

Buyer financing loan commitment or approval – The loan commitment or approval says "yes, we'll do the loan for this buyer on this home." Often there are conditions that have to be met to do this. The key is to understand this document and the conditions, if any, that appear on it. Clarification from the loan officer or mortgage broker is essential in determining any delays that may be caused by any of these conditions.

Inspection Report(s) – In the home inspection report you find a detailed description of the home, its issues, and photos.

Generally there is a summary of the issues that should be addressed as well. Depending on the property and the buyer there may be other inspections such as termite, septic, roof, pool, etc.

Appraisal – The appraisal is used by the lender to determine a fair market value of the property. In addition to the description of the home, photos are included, as well as a map of the area. The properties that are comparable to the subject home (the one being sold) are often called comps, which are detailed there as well based on recent sales and generally include photos.

Title Commitment – This is a commitment to insure from the title insurance company. There are three sections or schedules to the commitment. Schedule A is the description of the property, the proposed insured amount, and the proposed insured, as well as the effective date. Schedule B-1 is the description of what has to happen to issue the title policy. Generally there are routine items such as recording the appropriate instrument which transfers the title from seller to buyer and paying off any mortgages. If there are title issues, something that has to be resolved before closing, this is where they will be reflected. The final Schedule B-2 is the exceptions to the policy. These are the items that will not be insured. Generally they include easements, HOA covenants, and future taxes. It's wise to have someone fully explain this document to you, as well as provide you with copies of the exceptions for the buyer to review.

At Closing:

The following documents, along with a plethora of others, (depending on the loan type, lender, and the state) will show up at closing where the buyer is obtaining financing to purchase the home.

Back when I closed transactions it would take about an hour to go through the closing statement and the assorted lender docs. Buyers were often excited about the home they were purchasing and didn't question the documents very much, except for terms like their interest rate, payment amount, and length of the repayment period. Occasionally, we'd get a buyer who read each and every word.

While I found it frustrating at the time, I now have absolute respect for them and their desire to verify what they are getting themselves into. In most situations the documents are federal forms and don't vary from lender to lender with the exception of a few lender specific affidavits.

Note – The note is basically an IOU. It says you promise to pay back the amount borrowed, with interest, at the agreed upon terms spelled out in the note. It's a negotiable instrument and the original always goes to the lender. When the loan is paid in full it should be returned and marked "Paid in Full" to the borrower.

Mortgage – This is a voluntary lien that secures the note and the repayment of the debt pledging the home as collateral. In different parts of the country there are different names for this instrument; sometimes it's called a mortgage deed.

Loan Estimate (formerly called the TIL or Truth In Lending Disclosure Statement – This is designed to show you the estimated total costs of borrowing, the expected payment amounts over the life of the loan, and other significant elements of your loan. There are four sections of this form I want to point out. The first is the Annual Percentage Rate, or APR. This is the cost of your loan expressed as a yearly rate. The second is the Finance Charge. This is the dollar amount the loan will cost you. Next, the Amount Financed is the amount of credit provided to you or on your behalf. Lastly, you have the Total of Payments, which is the amount you will have paid after making all payments as scheduled. The purpose of an APR is to allow you to quickly compare the total costs between competing loans without having to analyze all of the individual costs within each loan.

Amortization Schedule – This is simply a schedule showing when payments are made and what portion of them is applied to the interest, principal, and the remaining principal balance due. A portion of each payment goes toward both principal and interest, and each time a payment is made the amount applied to principal changes. Early in the life of the loan, the amount applied to the principal is very small and as the payments progress this number goes up.

As mentioned earlier, there is a vast amount and a wide variety of documents that go into getting a seller's home sold and a buyer into it. In various states they are prepared by different individuals. For instance, in much of New York, where I've had several clients who have my team coordinate their transactions, there is a purchase memo outlining the terms the buyer and seller have agreed to. That is sent to the buyer's and seller's attorneys, then later they actually sign the contract.

Contrary to that, in Florida for instance, the contract is prepared, as are the disclosures and addenda generally, by the agent who is representing the buyer when making the offer.

Of course as a licensed agent, you've been trained on which documents to use, for which transactions, and such. The key I want to convey to you here is to ask for help if you're unsure which documents are to be used for a particular transaction.

To save time, be sure to check the documents for missing signatures, dates, or initials while the transaction is in its early stages.

Final note – Keep copies, preferably digitally, backed up with your favorite backup system, so that you can access them if you should ever need to. Laws vary by locations as to what needs to be retained and for how long; be sure to fully comprehend this and don't skip this important step. Just because the "fat lady" has sung and you've gotten your check doesn't mean it's time to be lazy.

"Small deeds done are better than great deeds planned." Peter Marshall

No act of kindness, no matter how small,
is ever wasted. Aesop

Chapter 5

COMMUNICATION

One of the biggest complaints in most relationships is that one party doesn't feel like he/she is being heard. I believe that communication isn't really about telling someone or several some ones what is happening, it's about making sure that they understand it, they have time to have their questions answered, and "feel" as if they are being heard when they speak.

There is a quote by Maya Angelou that sums this up: "people will often forget what you tell them, but they will never forget how you made them feel." Since most businesses, especially real estate, are referral driven, it makes perfect sense to do what you can to make those you're communicating with feel good.

There are countless books on effective communication in the workplace and in our personal relationships; many of those books I've read and learned something helpful. At the end of the day, however, it all boils down to one simple thing: it's not what you do, it's how the other person feels that will determine their satisfaction or dissatisfaction with the sale/purchase of a home with you.

If you've got some time, there is a great video on TED (Ted.com) by Rob Legato titled *The Art of Creating Awe.*

"When we're infused with either enthusiasm or awe or fondness … it changes what we see. It changes what we remember." (Rob Legato)

In the video, Rob does an excellent job of showing us how as a movie producer he uses special effects to create an experience for the viewer.

In our business it's important that we remember that it's not what happened, it's how the other person interpreted it that will impact the feelings they have when recalling the event.

This section is broken down into several sections and sub-sections. There are scripts as well as email suggestions to make your job easier.

   a.   <u>Communication with the buyer and/or seller</u>: How to effectively stay in contact with them to build trust and referrals.

   b.   <u>Communication with the Realtor</u>: How to effectively stay in contact so that there are no issues with your client's closing.

   c.   <u>Communication with the lender, title company, and other key parties to the transaction</u>: Knowing what questions to ask and what to listen for can often make the difference between a smooth closing and a train wreck. This section will guide you through the process.

As I've mentioned before, residential real estate is loaded with ups and downs. I'm not going to sugarcoat this or tell you what you think you may want to hear; at some point you will be dealing with difficult people or difficult situations. This business can get really messy and it can often be extremely challenging. Here are a few things to say when you just aren't sure what or how to say it:

- ☐ I can appreciate how you feel.
- ☐ I understand how you feel. If I were in your shoes, I would probably feel the same.
- ☐ Can you please explain you why you feel that way?
- ☐ I see your point of view.

- ☐ I understand.
- ☐ Please tell me about...
- ☐ Let me make sure I completely understand. (repeat and rephrase their statements)

Always smile when you speak.

I believe that professionalism is a must. Some gurus will disagree with me, saying that you should play naive when making offers or communicating with others, but it's my opinion that this is deceitful. Additionally, you are running a business; you should let everyone know at every opportunity that this is what you do. It's called ABM, Always Be Marketing. Either you're marketing to people and they are thinking they'd like to do business with you or they are thinking, "What a jerk!"

Letting the folks you talk with, email with, or meet with know you're a pro will help you build your business. That doesn't mean you have to know everything; I assure you after 20 or so years and being part of over 100,000 transactions, I still learn something on a regular basis. That's what makes it *fun* and interesting.

There are many different types of transactions you can and will be doing in your business. Most have the same or similar elements: a buyer, a seller, closing agent, and often a lender. Depending on the transaction, you may be the seller and the lender, or you may be the buyer, or the wholesaler accepting an assignment fee.

Each transaction will be unique and you'll want to adapt the information that follows to meet the needs of your transaction.

Initiating communication

I suggest that at the beginning you introduce yourself to everyone – the title agent, attorney, mortgage broker or lender, other Realtor, etc. If you establish a good rapport at the onset of a transaction with these parties and others involved, it will make the transaction run that much more smoothly for all involved. Let them know who you are, what your role in the transaction is, and that you're ready to help if needed to do what it takes to get a transaction closed. If you have an assistant or a transaction coordinator they should do this on your behalf.

Years ago when I worked at a law firm doing closings, I received a strange call one day from a Realtor who was calling to confirm his sales commission. I wasn't sure who he was as I'd never heard his name mentioned before and I politely told him so. I placed him on hold and pulled the file. While he was on hold I reviewed the file which I'd had for six weeks or so now preparing for closing. I saw no mention of him in the file or on the sales contract, at the time the agents were not mentioned on contracts in Florida. I explained this to him and he said, "That's okay, I guess you didn't need me or you would have found me". Hmm… not what I was thinking, but anyway, it seemed that he was the seller's agent and was due a sales commission. He was calling to make sure we were planning to FedEx his check to him. I consulted the seller, who was our client and he said, "Yeah, I guess I forgot to mention that". Needless to say, had the agent not called the day before closing, he might not have gotten paid. For six weeks our file showed no agent and that the deal was a FSBO. His call meant we had to revise the closing statement, re-circulate it for approval, and amend the seller's proceeds amount.

Don't let this happen to you. Be involved, but not annoying. Learning to do this effectively comes with experience, and of course, education.

Let's break down communication into key roles of participants in the transaction.

Communicating with your seller client

Each seller is going to be unique. The seller who is selling the home they live in will have different challenges and expectations than the experienced investor seller or a seller who is being transferred or moving to a bigger house. No matter what I believe, it is up to you to set the stage for how you want the transaction to proceed. This goes back to being the professional.

To help you set this stage you'll want to use the seller contract to close informational sheet. You can find out where to get an editable copy of this in the resources section of this book. This information sheet has several components that are addressed briefly here:

- ☐ Hours of operation: Here is where you put your contact info and also the days and times you're available. I believe that in real estate transactions there isn't much that needs to be done, if anything, after normal business hours. You decide what works best for you.

- ☐ The next sections outline the accessibility of the home for inspections, appraisal, survey, etc.

- ☐ The final sections discuss closing, what to expect and that all parties involved need to attend.

If this is the only home your seller has sold, or if it's been a while, this will be very helpful in providing them answers to common real estate matters as they apply to their sale.

A few words of caution when working with sellers of distressed properties:

1. Be involved: maintain communication but don't try to fix everything to make the deal close. At the risk of this sounding harsh, please remember you're in the real estate business.

2. Some sellers have other financial problems other than paying their mortgage. If you find yourself investing in an area where this is happening often, you may find a resource or two of local community agencies that help displaced or troubled homeowners that you can pass on. Other than that, you'll need to just maintain your focus on the transaction at hand and be as pleasant and patient as possible.

3. Some distressed transactions are a result of divorce. *These can be particularly ugly.* Once, I worked on a deal where I was the closing agent, and the sellers were clearly still *very* angry with one another. Actually, I think angry is an understatement. At the closing table they argued and argued and continued to get very loud with one another across the table over the fees on closing statement. At one point the male reached across the table and smacked his hand on the papers the female had in front of her. Sadly, they were arguing over less than $45.00, which I would have gladly paid to make them stop, but they were clearly using this as an excuse to continue to argue as they had been for a while. I excused myself from the room to give them some time to work it out alone but that didn't help. Soon after I walked away they were out in the street in the middle of downtown Orlando screaming at each other. In the end the police came and gave them two options, stop it or go risk going to jail. They came back in, signed, and received their proceeds. The woman called me afterward and apologized; she was embarrassed and felt bad for putting me into that situation.

Note: No matter the situation or circumstance, just treat everyone with dignity, kindness, and compassion.

Communicating with the buyer

As you can imagine, buyers are all different as well. They come in many shapes and sizes. Some of the buyers you'll work with may be first time home buyers. While they are often the neediest in terms of information on the process, and wanting to communicate often, I've also found they are generally the easiest to work with. Some of the buyers you work with may be move-up buyers or second home buyers. They may have purchased a home or two in the past. Then the other buyer you'll routinely work with is the frequent buyer, the investor buyer who is maybe in the fix-and-flip business, or is a buy-and-hold investor who has multiple rentals in his portfolio.

Similar to the seller contract to close informational sheet, you may find using the buyer version very helpful. This information sheet has several components that are addressed briefly here:

1. Hours of operation: Here is where you put your contact info and also the days and times you're available. You decide what works best for you.

2. The next sections outline financing. This is simply a glossary to help the buyer understand the process.

3. Inspections, insurance, and utilities are covered to help remind the buyer to take care of these items in a timely manner.

☐ The final sections discuss closing, what to expect, and that all parties involved need to attend.

You may find the information sheets useful as prepared and only need to add your contact information and hours of operation. You may also decide to modify or add information helpful to the buyers or sellers in the area you're investing in. One coaching client of mine who uses these forms adds a sheet to the back of it as well, for the buyer and/or seller to have a place to make notes and add the contact information for the closing agent. In today's digital age you could also use these as an email that you send rather than a piece of paper you give to someone.

Note to real estate investors: Remember, if the buyer or seller is represented by a Realtor or attorney, your communication will go through their representative.

The mortgage broker or loan officer

The loan is a critical part of the real estate buying and selling process. I've always said "he who has the money makes the rules," and while this may be true, it doesn't mean that they don't need help along the way. Over the years, obtaining financing has become more challenging. Knowing every step of the way and what to watch out for is *critical*. Remember- **no one gets paid, until something closes.** Therefore, when you are calling on the lender, mortgage broker, or buyer's agent to determine the status of the loan, you have to ask specific questions. *"Fine"* or *"okay"* when asking about the status is never a good answer; often it's a sign of something going wrong and them not wanting to tell you. Several key questions will give you the big picture on the pulse of the loan. Here are some suggestions:

> **Has the buyer finalized their application?** While in most cases the buyer will continue to use the lender that they have met with to obtain their pre-approval, sometimes this isn't the case. I'm of the trust but verify mindset, trust that the buyer has applied, and that you have the information correct on who they are working with to obtain financing and *verify* that this info you have is accurate. When calling to introduce yourself to the lender and verify the buyer has applied, you can

also set the stage for the lender to let them know you'll be checking in and there if they should need anything.

Has the appraisal been ordered? This is a valid question and can often determine if the broker/lender feels they can complete the loan. If no appraisal has been ordered, soon after the contract has been executed it's important to find out why and equally important when it will be completed. If there is an issue with the property appraising at or above contract price, it's best to find that out as early as possible so that a solution to this problem can be found.

When will you have the loan commitment? In most sales contracts, the buyer and seller have already agreed upon a time whereby the loan commitment will be delivered. It's very critical to get the loan commitment as soon as possible. After receiving the loan commitment, review it closely. Ask the lender, mortgage broker, or buyer's agent questions on any of the conditions you don't fully understand.

If there is something kooky on the loan commitment, like documentation from a long lost relative or past employer that has ceased operations, you may have a challenge on your hands. The sooner you know this, the better it is to deal with it.

 Bright Idea Do not wait until the day the loan commitment is due to start calling on it. I've taught my team to call a few days before the loan commitment is due, to give themselves time to get in touch with the lender and also to let the lender know they are serious about getting it timely.

How will you handle clearing these conditions? Ask if they've contacted the buyer, title company, appraiser, or whoever will be responsible for getting the information needed. When do they expect to have this information delivered? And also ask if they anticipate issues in getting *any* of these items.

When do you expect the "clear to close"? The "clear to close" indicates that the loan is fully approved and the lender is ready to prepare the loan docs for closing. Some title companies and attorneys will not schedule a closing without knowing the loan is clear to close. The sooner that this is available, the better!

When will the loan packet be delivered to the closing agent? Having the loan packet early will allow time for the title company or attorney to prepare the closing statement and circulate it for changes and approval.

Lending laws recently changed with the Dodd Frank Act require that the closing statement—now called closing disclosure—be given to the buyer three days prior to the closing date. Having seen more than my fair share of evening closings with West coast lenders who get loan docs delivered digitally at the last minute, not giving the buyer time to fully understand what they are signing, I believe it's a good thing. I recall one specific closing where the buyer pulled up with everything they owned in a U-Haul truck, their mortgage broker met them at the closing which was originally scheduled for 2pm that day, but with the lender not doing their part to make that happen, it ended up being at 7pm on a Friday. While reviewing the documents the buyer questioned the fees and the mortgage broker said (and I quote) "this is the best we can do, I know it's not what I promised you but in a few years once the equity has gone up in your home you can refinance and even take out some of the equity you'll have built up." This took place in 2004 and sure, at that time, home values were on the upswing, and we all know that just a few years later this was not the case.

I've often wondered about that buyer and if they were able to keep the home or if because this mortgage broker lied and they felt like they had no option if they ended up losing it like so many others did.

There are many strategies used to market a home and bring in the buyers. However, if the person handling the financing isn't pulling their weight, you're headed for a bumpy road and sometimes a very disappointing experience. Putting the deal together is just half of the battle, keeping it together and getting it to close is the other half.

Remember: As I mentioned above, introduce yourself at the onset of the transaction to the person handling the financing. Be sure they have your contact information as well as a complete copy of the contract and *all* addenda. I suggest you call the person who signed the pre-approval letter you received as part of the offer as well, either upon receipt of the offer, or at the latest once the offer is negotiated. Your call should go something like this:

Hi, this is _____. I see that you've met with Mr. and/or Ms. Buyer about buying the home I have for sale. (Wait to hear his reply; you'll get a lot from his tone and how quickly he responds to your inquiry) I'm the seller's agent/transaction coordinator (or seller if this is a FSBO/investor) and I just wanted to introduce myself as well as make sure I had the correct contact info for you to pass along to the closing agent. Do you prefer phone or email correspondence? (At this time ask him for email, fax, etc.) Great, I'll send you a copy of the contract as well as the closing agent's info in a short while. My contact info will be in there, so please let me know if I can be of any assistance.

Thanks for your time.

Now you'll want to send this person a complete copy of the contract along with the Transaction Summary, which will have all the current contact information on it for everyone thus far in the deal.

Here's the suggested email and/or content:

Subject: Financing for {Buyer Name} purchase of {Project Description}

Dear {Lender Representative Name}:

Attached you will find the transaction summary information and the executed sales contract along with addenda. Please confirm that {Buyer Name}, the buyer of the above referenced home, has applied for financing. When the appraisal report is in, please confirm with me that the property wasn't appraised at or above the contracted price.

Additionally, please provide me with the loan commitment letter on or before the agreed upon date of _____, in the sales contract.

If you have any questions or if I can be of any assistance, please do not hesitate to contact me.

Thank you,

Your Signature

The Closing Agent

Depending on where you are working, the closing agent may be called something else like escrow officer, title agent, closing attorney, etc. In some states closings are handled by attorneys, in others they are handled by escrow officers. In all cases, what I am referring to in this section is communicating with the person who will decide if everything is ready for closing.

The closing agent will either handle the title search and issue the title insurance, or in some places will work together with a title company. In most transactions, however, you will have only one or two people in that office you'll communicate with in respect to closing and title. Generally the file is assigned to a processor who will handle making sure that a title search is ordered. He or she will be the person who will communicate with the mortgage side for the seller to obtain the necessary payoff information to satisfy any mortgage(s) encumbering the property. She will also be communicating with the buyer's mortgage professional to provide them with the necessary title commitment and other supporting documents to facilitate the approval of the loan.

If there is an HOA or condo associate, she will call and get the necessary fees to be included on the closing statement when it's prepared. If there are title issues that need to be resolved, the processor will also be the one generally making calls to cure those issues.

NOTE: if there is a title issue do not assume that the title agent is working full speed to resolve it. They are busy and juggles many files at once. If there is an issue, offer to help or at the very least check in often to see how it's going in clearing it.

When all the title requirements are met and the loan documents have arrived (or at least the closing figures from the lender), then the file is assigned to the closer who will take it the rest of the way and meet with the buyer and seller to sign the documents.

I always advise that you do everything you can to make the title agent's processor your *best friend*. She's the one who will help make sure all the "i's" are dotted and the "t's" are crossed. She will also be an invaluable resource in answering questions on how the process works in that specific part of the country. If you're unsure about anything or need information, she will help you on this transaction and likely on others you are putting together.

Communicating at the onset of a transaction with the closing agent is key. Once you have the correct contact information for the person who will handle the closing, pick up the phone and call them. Here's a suggested dialog for communicating with a new company:

"Hi, my name is _____. I am the seller/investor/Realtor/transaction coordinator to a transaction that I understand your office will be handling. I've heard great things about your company and am looking forward to a smooth closing. I want to send you some information to help you as well as my contact information. Would you prefer I email this or fax it, and to whose attention should I address this?"
Once you have jotted down the contact info, thank them and tell them what you're sending other than the contract, and ask there will be anything else needed at this moment to get the process rolling.

When you're communicating with a title company you've worked with in the past, it's still important that you pick up the phone, alert them to the new transaction, then follow-up with the email or fax of the information. Your call should go something like this:

"Hi, it's _____. Great news! We're going to do another transaction together. I just wanted to alert you that it's on the way. I'll email you the details in just a moment."

In chapter 6 I discuss file documentation and I've given you some ideas on forms to use to track and communicate with the title company.

Here's the suggested email and/or content for your fax coversheet—the Transaction.

Subject: Title Order Confirmation for {Project Description}

Dear {title agent name or the processor}:

I am the *(seller, investor, buyer, agent, transaction coordinator, etc.)*. Your company has been selected as the closing agent for this transaction. I'm looking forward to working with you.

Attached you will find the transaction summary information as well as the sales contract and addenda. At your earliest opportunity, please provide me with the title commitment for review.

I look forward to a smooth transaction and closing.

If I can be of further assistance or if you have any questions, you may contact me via email at _____ or by phone at _____.

Best wishes,

Your Signature

Throughout the transaction you'll be communicating with multiple parties in the deal. I'm of the school that you can catch more flies with honey than you can with vinegar. It's always good to establish relationships with people and companies in that area that can help you; you never know when down the road you may meet them again at another transaction or need to call on them to help you. Here are a few ways that will likely get you top priority on all your deals as well as get your questions answered quickly:

1. Send thank you cards after closing and perhaps send a small gift card if you think they've done an outstanding job. Many of the coordinators in my office routinely receives gift cards. They work hard and go the extra

mile for all our clients, but the cards really fuel them and affirm their hard work is truly appreciated.

2. Bring a gift to closing for the closing agent and/or office. Donuts, cookies, and candy are *cheap*; taking the time and initiative to do it is priceless.

3. Flowers. I don't think I have to explain much here. Once after a particularly challenging transaction, one of my clients sent me a dozen long stem roses as a thank you for all the extra hard work I'd done to make sure her deal closed. I still remember that when she calls. It's been about nine years and I'm still thinking of it. Yes, I answer her emails extremely fast and always take her calls.

While I'm a huge fan of email to ensure that there is documentation, often it can actually make things take longer. In my office I challenged our team to ramp up their phone communications as a test to see how effective it was. Also, I felt it would give the extra level of service we're know for even more.

In a month they called to give updates, rather than using email. At the end of the month we all found something very interesting:

It took far less time to get the information they needed and they got complete answers when they picked up the phone and connected. The team agreed that they initially thought email was easier, however after a month of challenging themselves to dial rather than send, they found that their work was easier and more rewarding.

Shocking, I know, for all my techie pals, but truth be told this business is about people; relationships and communication is a critical part of its success.

My final note on communication is to remember that almost everyone involved wants the same thing, a smooth closing.

However, some work styles and personalities will be far different than yours or what you'd expect. Don't be quick to judge or get angry. Be very friendly, firm when necessary, and as stated above, *always smile*, even when you're on the phone and want to come through it and choke the person on the other end of the line.

"Courteous treatment will make a customer a walking advertisement." J. C. Penney

"It is not the going out of port, but the coming in that determines the success of a voyage." Henry Ward Beecher

Chapter 6

CHECKLISTS, FORMS AND EMAIL TEMPLATES, OH MY!

Okay, here's where the geek comes out. This isn't the sexiest part of the business; as a matter of fact, as I've stated before, it's the part that we go through to simply get what we want. It's essential that you fully comprehend it *and* that you figure out ways to smart cut, similar to short cut, but smarter.

Other training materials you probably are already familiar with or own provide you with the systems you need to successfully identify properties, marketing, negotiating, and getting a deal under contract. Very few cover the information in this book, or specifically how to create a system to streamline the contract to close a portion of your business.

If you don't already have an office manual for your business, I encourage you to take small steps daily to create one. If you're new to real estate, you may be thinking, "office manual? I just want to make some money!" The idea of doing it all yourself may sound appealing, and creating an office manual for something you're not even sure how to do is a far off idea. But as soon as you get going in this business, you'll see that there are certain things you do regularly, such as emails you send, conversations you have, etc., which all can be incorporated into an office manual. If you've been in this business for a while, you're already there; now it's time to document it.

In Chapter 3 of this book I covered the importance of creating systems and how to do it for your business, so I won't go back over them here. Of course if you're stumped there, sign up for one of my workshops and I'll happily help guide you through the process of creating effective systems for your business.

In this chapter and the subsequent sub-chapters I'm going to outline some of the items that you should be tracking from contract to close as well as how to effectively do this.

One of the first things you'll need is to have a handy place where all the info is together. A place where you or someone you're working with can quickly see the details of a transaction and what needs to be done when to get it closed smoothly. A system to make sure that no details are overlooked and that the transaction flows smoothly. I'm a big fan of doing this digitally and in the resource section of this book you'll find several online programs that can help you.

I do *not* recommend trying to do this without a net. By that I mean trying to manage a transaction without a system. And for the record, saying a prayer and crossing your fingers once you have a fully executed contract is *not* a system. One of the most common frustrations I hear from Realtors and investors is that they are simply overwhelmed. My first advice is for them to stop coordinating their transactions and delegate that to an expert, **hint, hint, TMC, my company, does that for smart people like you.** However, I understand that not everyone who needs help is ready to let go and delegate, so the information in this chapter will walk you or even your assistant through keeping up with a file from contract to close.

Transaction Summary and Checklist

The first form we'll be discussing is the transaction checklist. This is designed to help you streamline your business. This is what we use at TMC to coordinate thousands and thousands of transactions each year. Of course, we customize it, as you should for the uniqueness of your market, your style of doing things, as well as the contract itself.

This checklist is the *road map* for making sure that everything that needs to be done is handled, and it will also help you track dates. Of course, checklists are only as helpful as the information you put onto them. By taking just a few minutes, generally less than fifteen, when you first put your deal together, to pull out the info needed, you'll save so much time during the process as well as prevent any unfortunate or costly mistakes.

NOTE: Any items that don't apply to your transaction should be crossed out when you are compiling this form. This will prevent confusion as your deal progresses.

Transaction Summary

The transaction summary form is where you keep all the essential information of the contract together in one concise place. Most transaction coordinating software programs will have these place holders for information and allow you to customize other fields that are applicable to your location. I recommend that you confirm that you can print out the summary info into a form that you can share with others in the transaction to save you time.

The goal here is to have a place where you can reference the important info at a glance and the dates certain actions are due. Completed either by you or your transaction coordinator as you gather information about the other parties, it's a reference place to quickly contact anyone involved in the transaction and get the information needed.

One time saver is to send it along with the sales contract to the title company, lender, 1031 exchange company, and anyone else necessary. I know some people who also print this and keep it in a notebook in case they are where they have no internet access and can't look up the details online.

Here's how using the form described above can save you an extreme amount of time in a deal. Say you send this form originally to the title company, but haven't yet learned who the 1031 exchange company will be. Later you find this out and update your form. Most of us would be tempted to call the title agent and give them the information, and while I think talking with people is essential in building rapport and getting the info you need, it's not always the most efficient, as you'll see from how a call to update the title agent may go:

Ring, ring.

"Hello – ABC Title, how can I direct your call?"

"Hi, this is Michelle; is Sally the closer available?"

"She's on another line" the receptionist tells you, "would you like to hold a minute? I don't think she'll be long."

"Sure" you say; you've already called and may as well get this done and crossed off your list.

(Hold music…) After a minute she transfers you to Sally.

"Hi, this is Sally, how can I help you?"

"Hi Sally, it's Michelle Spalding, how are you today?"

"Great, thanks for asking, and you?"

"I'm doing very well, thank you. I've got the 1031 exchange information you need for the contract for 555 Main Street."

"Thanks, Michelle, hang on a second, let me get the file (or open the file on my computer)" (more hold music…)

"Okay, Michelle, go ahead."

Next you proceed to give her the name, contact name, phone, address and email information. You exchange goodbyes and end the call. Total time—several minutes or longer. Not a big deal, right? Especially since you already have heard me talk about the importance of communication and building rapport with others involved.

However, on items like this I suggest that you just fax or email the form instead, taking only about thirty seconds to do either. Then you don't have to hold, make idle chit chat and wait for her to jot down the info you just received. Worse yet, you don't have to receive a call later after you've left the office asking you to confirm the phone number for the 1031 exchange company as Sally says, "I must have written it down incorrectly."

Everywhere you can save time, you can use that to do more of the things you want.

Transaction Checklists

The document checklist below is one that our office uses for each transaction. We have custom versions we've created for our clients, based on their individual business and we also modify it for each transaction, deleting some things and adding others, depending on what the contract calls for.

As you can see this is a fairly large list of documents that need to be compiled. Some will be required by your office, some will not and yet are equally as important. Most firms will not require the title commitment for instance, but you should obtain a copy and see to it that your buyer gets it.

A checklist is designed to help you take the things that need to happen out of your head and put them into a place where you can easily see what has been completed and what you or your transaction coordinator need to get.

Date Received	Document
	Contract Documents
	Sales contract
	Addendum
	Disclosure Documents
	Agency disclosure (if applicable)
	Seller's disclosure
	Mold disclosure
	HOA disclosure or condo disclosure
	Lead-based paint warning statement
	Inspection Reports
	Termite inspection
	Home inspection (or waiver)
	Appraisal
	Title & Escrow Documents
	Tax information report
	Property appraiser report
	Copy of deposit check
	Receipt for deposit
	Closing instructions
	Survey
	Title commitment
	Estimate of closing costs
	Final closing statement
	Final signed closing statement
	Executed deed
	Loan Documents
	Buyer's pre-qualification letter
	Loan commitment letter
	Other Documents
	Hazard insurance
	Contract to close buyer or seller
	Transaction summary
	Directions to title company
	MLS report
	Home warranty confirmation
	Receipts for repairs (if applicable)
	Invoices for closing agent

On the following pages you'll find a checklist of the many tasks that need to be completed along the way to closing. Some may apply, some may not, but you'll see that I've included some suggested dates on when you should do these and also left some blank as they will be dictated by the contract.

Many tasks are the same or very similar whether you're on the buyer side of the transaction or the seller side as a Realtor. Likewise, if you're the buyer or seller as a real estate investor. You'll see under the transaction tasks section I have broken out some that are seller or buyer specific.

In any transaction you are only as strong as your weakest link, so even if you're on the seller side of a transaction, if the buyer's agent has checked out, you still need to know how the loan is progressing, so you'll have to reach out to the lender directly. I think this is a good idea anyway, as it's always better to have the information that can affect the closing first hand, rather than maybe watered down by a well-meaning buyer's agent.

If you are not using an online program to help you manage your transactions you should figure out the dates these items are due and then add them to your calendar. For some item, like the loan commitment and inspection deadline, I recommend you set the date they are due on your calendar and then a reminder a day or so before to give yourself a cushion to get them handled by the date the contract calls for.

If you have a transaction coordinator helping you, they should calculate all of the dates then share this with you, so you are fully aware of when the tasks are due. Your transaction coordinator should also notify you when these milestones are accomplished or when they run into an issue where one will not be done on time: but not at 5pm on the day it's due!

Task	Deadline
Contingency Removal	
Inspection deadline	
Deadline for buyer to report issues with inspe	
Receive buyer's commitment/approval letter	
Confirm appraisal acceptable to lender	
Contract	
Review contract documents–ensure fully exec and complete	1 day after start
Deposit or Earnest Money	
Verify deposit, obtain written confirmation (receipt)	
Verify additional deposit; obtain written confirmation (receipt)	
Disclosures	
Confirm all disclosures received and fully exe and complete	
Home Warranty	
Order or verify Home Warranty ordered	7 days before closing
Send copy of Home Warranty invoice to closing agent	7 days before closing
Inspections	

Reminder to buyer to select home and termite inspectors	1 days after start
Confirm inspection appointments with all parties via email	3 days after start
Schedule pre-closing walk-through with all parties and confirm via email	5 days before closing
Lender	
Verify buyer applied for financing	1 days after start
Verify with lender property appraised at or above value	10 days after start
Verify all conditions cleared with lender	7 days before closing
Pre-Closing	
Instructions to title company with regards to Realtor's commission	7 days before closing
Send any invoices to title agent for the closing statement	7 days before closing
File review with title co., lender to confirm clear too close	7 days before closing
Coordinate closing time and send directions to client	7 days before closing
Verify loan package received by title co./attor	4 days before closing
Obtain closing statement for review	3 days before closing date
Transaction Tasks	
Initiate contact with listing agent transaction coordinator, if applicable	1 days after start
Congrats we're under contract email to buyer or seller (introducing your team if you have one)	1 days after start

	Initiate contact with lender	1 days after start
	Confirm appraisal ordered with Lender	7 days after start
	Request utility information from seller and/or seller's agent	10 days after start
	Email title company to verify they have information needed from seller to close	15 days after start
	Provide utility information to buyer and/or buyer's agent	15 days after start
	Receive title commitment and send to buyer	10 days before closing
	Register buyer/seller up for Lowe's Realtor Benefits program	7 days before closing
	Email reminder to buyer/seller to schedule utility change and change of address	5 days before closing
	Schedule pre-closing walk through and send email to all parties confirming	5 days before end
	Transaction Tasks (Buyer specific)	
	Obtain copy of survey (if applicable) and send to buyer	7 days before closing
	Reminder to client/buyer to start condo/HOA approval process	3 days after start
	Transaction Tasks (seller specific)	
	If seller will *not* attend closing, let closing agent know and find out what arrangements will need to be made, mail away, pre-sign, power of attorney, etc.	10 days after start
	Confirm closing agent has information needed from seller to obtain payoff from current lender (mortgages)	20 days before closing

	Post-closing	
	Obtain a copy of the fully executed closing statement	1 day after closing
	Send thank you letter to buyer/seller along with a copy of the final closing statement for tax time (and any other important documents)	1 day after closing
	Thank you letter or card to referral source	1 day after closing
	Close out file and archive	1 day after closing
	Add client to your CRM to maintain relationship with them	1 day after closing
	If you didn't get a testimonial and/or referrals from client–follow-up	10 days after closing

Transaction Communication Summary

Communication is key. Documentation of that communication is **critical** in keeping your sanity, and also in preventing possible misunderstandings and even litigation. When I was working as a paralegal, I was taught to write down everything and keep all correspondence. I still do this to this day on all the deals I work on and my team does as well, so that at any moment anyone on our team or the agent we're working for can instantly see what has been discussed, including emails. I can't tell you how many times– months or even years later– someone has called and asked me for a copy of something and I'm always delighted when I have it and can be of assistance.

When I was speaking at a real estate investor club a few years ago one of the members chimed in when I mentioned documentation. He told the group that several years prior he was called into court and when he presented the pages of documentation he had the judge was impressed, and even told him so. The case he was called to court for was finalized and he was victorious; he attributed his success to having this documentation. While going into court is never what we want, it's a part of life sometimes, and a possibility when you are in business, especially real estate.

One final thought on forms or software...

Forms and transaction coordinating software is only as good as the information you or your partner(s)/assistant enter. Keeping detailed records will enable you to quickly recall information and also share the work with others; think leverage.

Imagine, knowing the last conversation your partner(s)/assistant had with the seller, without having to pick up the phone and call your partner(s)/assistant. Or receiving an email when certain milestones are met such as appraisal ordered, inspections complete, loan commitment received, etc.

That my friends is a system and with planning and effort, you can have this in your business, if you want it.

"In the race to be get to closing, don't forget to enjoy the journey!" Michelle Spalding

"I've learned that people will forget what you said, people will forget what you did, but people will never forget how you made them feel." Maya Angelou

Chapter 7

MANAGING THE DETAILS

Just because the ink is dry on the contract doesn't mean it's time to celebrate yet. Sure, it's a good time to make sure you've got some Champagne on hand and put it in the fridge because hopefully soon you'll be able to raise a toast to another successful home sale.

I was at an office teaching a class on how to manage the details from contract to close several years ago. Most of the agents in the class were fairly new and had closed at least six transactions each. I went around the room and asked them about their system, checklist, or the software they used to keep the details straight. Not one agent had a system, one did have a method (which I don't think you can solely rely on)—he told me, he says a prayer daily, crosses his fingers, and hopes everyone else is doing their job. Everyone laughed and confessed they, too, use that method.

Okay, that may have worked for the six or so transactions he'd done so far, but I asked him if he thought he could sustain that for very long or even see growing his business with that method. Of course he said no, and so did each of the other agents in the room.

Sometimes, I think that we are so excited when we get a contract that, like a new baby we just want to give it love and watch it grow. While that excitement is a good thing, and I've had three children and now a grandchild, so I'm all for giving love and watching, I also know that you have to set boundaries and do your very best to keep connected with them to help them grow into happy healthy adults.

The same holds true with our transactions. Once they go under contract we have to stay in touch with everyone, make sure that the rules are being followed, and also give our buyers/sellers love so they will continue to be happy clients once closing has taken place.

I've said this many times, *you're only as strong as your weakest link*. If there is someone involved who is, as a former boss of mine frequently said, a slacker, then you or someone on your team has to keep the chain together.

One of the ways I think we do this is by setting the expectations at the very beginning with everyone involved, letting them know that you'll be involved, that you want this to be as smooth as possible, and that if at any time they need help, to pick up the phone or send an email. I think that the expectations conversation has to be a phone call, not an email, mainly because you can get a feel immediately for the person you're going to spend the next month or so working with that you can't get in an email.

You have to be proactive, stay a step or two ahead of the deadlines and the contingencies, and anticipate the questions and concerns your buyer or seller may have. By educating them, and keeping them informed about the process of what is happening along the way they will have confidence in your skills and ability. Even when things are looking shaky because the other side is having issues, your clients will know you're looking out for them and their best interest.

I'll say now that while most people in this business are great and do their job with the utmost care and diligence, and have the same expectations as you do for this going smoothly, there are those that don't follow through with actions to support that.

Many years ago one of the transaction coordinators on my team was working with an agent who had the listing side of a transaction. The buyer's agent was also the mortgage broker, and as soon as the ink was dry he became impossible to reach. Throughout the transaction the coordinator as well as the agent tried and tried to reach him, via email, phone, fax and text. It was if he'd fallen off the face of the earth, until he needed something like access to the home for the appraiser, or a copy of an addendum re-sent because he lost the one he'd received last week.

As the transaction progressed, the agent client of ours became more and more concerned as was the coordinator. There were several extensions that were needed and at the time there were more homes for sale than buyers able to get financing, so the seller extended, each time each of us feeling less and less confident about it ever closing.

One day, Oscar the mortgage broker/Realtor called and said the loan package was going out and we were closing today. Throughout the entire transaction he'd only surfaced a few times and now he wanted everyone to scramble because the loan program he'd put his client into expired today…and also, I believe, so that he'd get paid that day.

Thankfully, the title company was accommodating and pulled it off with a late, late day closing. The sellers were already out of the house and fortunately didn't have to do a scramble to get the moving truck there.

To this day, when we have a mortgage broker who is unresponsive or uncooperative, we call it an Oscar deal. No matter how many calls we made, how many emails or faxes, he simply didn't respond.

I tell you this as an example of what happens sometimes and how important it is to keep your buyer/seller updated and let them know that you're doing everything you can. In the end, the seller of this home wrote a raving review for the agent and mentioned the coordinator by name who had also helped with updates. Funny enough, the buyer also felt that he wasn't getting info and called the listing agent several times; hopefully, they remembered which agent was the professional when it was time for them to sell or recommend a Realtor to a friend.

While keeping on top of everyone and everything is what it takes, it also takes keeping calm and letting your client know that you're in control and doing the very best. While smooth closings are what we all strive for, they don't always happen.

After you or your transaction coordinator has set the expectations in the introduction calls, it's time to track when things need to happen and make sure that no details are overlooked. In the following chapter of this book I've given you checklists you can use online or on good old fashioned paper and I also remind you that those are only as good as the person who is using them and updating them.

By using checklists and a calendar, or an online software that gives you notifications, you can stay ahead of the deadlines. It's frustrating when you forget something and call for it at the end of the day only to find out that person has gone for the day. You can't expect that your email will be returned promptly, or that the client you send a document to will even check their email that day. You have to take the lead, pick up the phone and communicate. You have to manage the details; your clients are relying on you.

Now here's where I want to give you some friendly advice and this isn't the mother in me, it's something I've observed over years and years of doing this that works. You can get a lot more out of people when *you make them feel good about helping you, than you can by fussing at them*. Or as my Mama always says, "you can catch a whole lot more flies with honey than you can with vinegar." When you are calling, emailing, or texting be kind, be patient, and always ask for that person to help you get what you need, don't demand it. No one, not even you, likes being told what to do.

When I'm training new transaction coordinators this is one of the first lessons we go over—taking a sort of subservient role to the person you're calling, rather than a dominating role. *Even* if they told you'd they'd send it and haven't, even if they didn't reply to the last ten emails you sent, I tell them, always start off the conversation in situations like that with something like "Can you help me get this crossed off my list?" Or "Can you please send this over so my agent will stop asking me for it?"

Since none of us are perfect, the person you're trying to get information out of may actually be going through something really difficult in their personal life and not be at their best; yelling at them or getting angry will not make this situation better. They may also be totally careless and not be paying attention and yelling will not make the situation any better. Now, I'm going to go Mama on you and just say *"be nice,"* it works.

If your system to manage the details once you have transactions under contract is like the individuals in the class I was teaching, a prayer and then trying to remember everything, you are truly limiting yourself and doing a disservice to your clients and yourself. I agree that prayer is helpful, and so is focused action.

Earlier today before I sat down to write this chapter I was chatting with a woman who'd found out about TMC online and called our office. I asked her why she was interested in having a transaction coordinator to help her and she said "I need to get all this stuff out of my head, it's waking me up at night." She said she'd done a fairly good job juggling it, staying on top of things, and yet felt she could do better and also wanted better for her clients. She was two years into the business and had already closed more than sixty transactions.

When I told her about the white paper done by Clarity Consulting way back in 2003 that said it took about 19 hours for an agent to coordinate a transaction from contract to close, and that with our help she could probably get that down to about 4, she whipped out the calculator and did the math. At 15 hours per transaction times 60 and then divide by 8, which she said was her average number of working hours, she realized that if she'd had someone helping her manage the details she would have had over 110 days she could have used for something else. She also said she would have also slept better as well. Don't take my word for it, read the report here: http://goo.gl/8bpeFQ

Even if you choose to do it all yourself, my goal in this book and the information I've taught over the years is to help you find ways to streamline that, to make it easier for yourself, and to provide a better experience for your buyer or seller.

Managing the details from contract to close is important, it can't be left to chance or the others, and it's something that your client is relying on you to guide them through, to oversee and to communicate with them frequently and honestly. *Yes*, it's often a lot of work, *yes* it's frustrating, *yes*, there is a lot of things to keep track of, *not* everyone is cooperative and helpful, *not* everyone is nice and does what they say they will do. Sadly, that's sometimes part of the journey to the closing table. And yet at the end of it, when a buyer gets the keys to the home they wanted, or a seller signs the closing docs and receives their proceeds, what they will remember is how you made them feel during the process.

"Without *ambition* one starts nothing. Without *work* one finishes nothing. The prize will *not* be sent to you. You have to *win* it. The man who knows *how* will always have a job. The man who also knows *why* will always be his boss. As to *methods* there may be a million and then some, but principles are few. The man who grasps *principles* can successfully select his own methods. The man who tries methods, ignoring principles, is sure to have *trouble*." Ralph Waldo Emerson

Chapter 8

CLOSING = PAY DAY, RIGHT?

Closing is the goal we are all in this to accomplish.

It should truly be the time for celebration.

Truth be told, it's the easiest part of the whole thing when done right. It's simply when the seller signs the necessary documents to convey the property to the buyer. Where the seller receives the proceeds and where the buyer exchanges money for the keys. Easy breezy!

For most, it's the reward for the work, often hard work, it takes to get there. It's also where the seller is paid, in most situations. Closing is when the others involved in the transaction such as the title agent, Realtors, the mortgage broker, etc., receive their hard earned commission or fee.

When the ground work is laid and the work necessary to make it happen is complete, then you'll have a closing, preferably a smooth one. I've already discussed the need for getting everything together and keeping everyone moving along the way to achieve this goal in a previous chapter. Other than that, I will simply restate the need for getting everything done and worked out before you converge to the closing table.

I'm sure you'll agree that you want the kind of closing experience that will result in the buyer/seller sharing great comments about their experience. After all, buying a house is rather obvious to those acquainted with the buyer or seller. Unlike the bad experience that we may have in a shoe store or a restaurant, buying or selling a house is noticeable to many and one of the most common questions people receive when they move is "How'd it go for you buying/selling a house?" Here's the truth: if the transaction ended smoothly, that is what your client will remember. Sure, they may recall the struggle to get the seller to fix something or the buyer's challenge with financing, but when it comes down to it, if they simply showed up, signed some documents, and went on their merry way, *that* is what they will remember most.

I've been a part of tens of thousands of closings, both as a transaction coordinator as well as a paralegal for a law firm which handled strictly real estate transactions. As you can imagine, from sitting at the table with buyers and sellers as well as their respective agents, I've seen my fair share of mayhem. Much of this came from people who were still working out issues at the closing table or from people who didn't know what to expect.

What I've found in all of them is that there were two parties who agreed upon a certain set of terms in the contract who want this done as quickly, efficiently, and easily as possible. Most of the time this is what happens, and everyone is happy. I still have a pile of thank you cards and emails that I've received over the years from people who were thrilled with the process and thanking me for my part in it. When days are tough, and I'm ready to throw in the towel, I sometimes look at them to give myself a little pep needed to keep moving forward.

"Adversity is the trial of principle. Without it, a man hardly knows whether he is honest or not." Henry *Fielding*

While I may be a positive person and look for the best at all times, I am not naive and expect anyone to believe that all transactions will go smoothly if we just work hard. Crap happens, deals go sideways, and people are not always on their game. Sometimes they get messy and it takes skill, patience, and persistence to get through them. Many challenges that occur at closing are a result of people being uninformed or lied to.

I'm a firm believer in being truthful; as a matter of fact I will instantly fire or discontinue a relationship with someone who is untrustworthy. No exceptions! That said, no matter how tough things are, no matter how difficult it may feel for you, or how you think you'll help someone by "sparing" them the truth, you won't. Lies don't work; withholding information doesn't either, so suck it up, no matter what it is and be truthful.

I was once handling a closing, the seller had pre-signed or was coming by later to sign, I can't recall which, but do know that only the two young buyers were at the table along with their mortgage broker. As typical in a closing, the closing agent, me in this situation, reviews the figures with the buyer that are a part of the Closing Statement. We go over them line, by line, by line, or at least that was the way I was taught. So at this table I'm reviewing the lender fees and we get to the YSP or Yield Spread Premium, which on this transaction was well over $4,000. The buyer stopped me and asked me to explain it to him, which I did. Again, that was my job.

He looked across the table to his mortgage broker and said "I thought you were only receiving the $995 mortgage broker fee." At this moment, the mortgage broker literally kicked me under the table. I assure you it was no accident, he was angry that he'd been caught in a lie, and wanted me to know. I spoke up and asked the mortgage broker to explain this, as it was his fee, not mine, and I stepped away to grab a soda. When I returned the buyer indicated he wanted to continue, yet I could see he was not happy. I think he felt he had no choice, everything he owned was on a moving truck and he and his wife had to have a place to live. I am extremely confident that he and his wife never referred any further business to the lying mortgage broker.

Now before you think I'm opposed to people making money in this business let me stop you. If you've consulted with your client and he/she has agreed to pay a fee, then fine, but don't think you can lie and have a long and prosperous business.

Sure, this mortgage broker may have thought the buyer would never notice it, or painted it as something it wasn't in order to get them to the closing table. Any of that is a lie and when that happens it runs the risk of deals blowing up at the table.

In another unpleasant closing, I recall a seller who was unaware of FIRPTA and its effects on their proceeds. I won't bore you with the details of FIRPTA, but I will say that if a foreign seller is unaware of it or its implications they will be *very* mad at their Realtor come closing, as I believe they should be.

In this particular situation, the sellers really needed the entire amount of the proceeds to purchase a home somewhere else. They'd committed to it, and left a sizable deposit to assure the seller they'd be back to conclude the transaction. With them now being about $30,000 short, the wife was beside herself and literally "lost her lunch" in the nearby trash can.

There were moments in both of those experiences where I thought that one of those parties was going to call the deal off. Where they were going to simply call it quits, go back to where they came from and walk away from this transaction. I've seen that happen and it's not pretty.

Had the parties involved been truthful, not withheld critical information, made the time to educate their clients or have others who were knowledgeable consult with them, the entire experience at the table would have been entirely different. It would have also been a lot more pleasant and the closing would have been more of a celebration rather than a sucker punch.

Soon after I opened up TMC, one of my clients and I got to chatting about closings and how he liked his handled. As his coordinator, he wanted me to let the title agent know that he'd be bringing Champagne, petit fours, as well as balloons. He wanted his clients and the rest of the team at closing to celebrate the accomplishment. I love this idea and hope that you'll take some element of it into your business and make the goal of closing a celebration. Perhaps not with Champagne, but then again, maybe so.

As the professional in a real estate transaction, it's up to us to do our very best in guiding our clients through the process. There is no way to know when you first take a buyer shopping or list a home what will happen. For gosh sakes, if Realtors had crystal balls that would show them what was around the corner I can bet many deals that they participated in would have not been so. Along the way to closing, many obstacles can, and often do, come up. The professional who is honest, compassionate, and on top of the transaction will no doubt have happy clients who will refer others to them.

As you navigate the path from contract to close with your client, enjoy the journey along the way, get people to help you where possible and when you arrive at closing, relax, celebrate, and have fun. You've all earned it.

"In business, one of the challenges is making sure that your product is the easiest to experience and complete a sale." Mark Cuban

"Business is not just doing deals; business is having great products, doing great engineering, and providing tremendous service to customers. Finally, business is a cobweb of human relationships." H. Ross Perot

Chapter 9

FISHING FOR REFERRALS & WHAT YOU SHOULD KEEP FOR YOUR FILE(S)

Once the deal is closed, many of us are tempted to stuff the file in a cabinet and hope to never look at it again. This is especially true if it's been a stressful transaction. While you may never need all or even part of the contents of the file in the future, tidying it up and making sure you have everything is not a waste of your time should the need arise to access it again.

Seeking testimonials and referrals while the deals are still fresh is always the best time. Get them while they are in the euphoria of having just reached their goal with your help. You were part of them buying or selling a home, which for most is one of the biggest things that happen in life.

Put that experience to use to generate more like it.

Get out your fishing pole and start fishing.

As a business owner, (yes, as a Realtor or real estate investor you are a business owner) you have to *Always Be Marketing*. If you want to build a successful business, you have to continually let others know what you do and how you can possibly help them. What challenges people faced, and the solutions you offered to allow your client to overcome them. There are countless books, programs, and information on marketing, so I'm not going to get into that in this book. What I intend to cover are two marketing approaches as they relate directly to the closing that just took place. I'm also going to cover how to get this done for you by someone else if you're not at closing.

Post-closing survey

You can find a sample of the post-closing feedback summary form in the resources page of this book.

The post-closing feedback summary can help you gauge how others on your team are doing. For instance, if you have been referring a lot of your buyers to "Bob the Mortgage Broker," and getting negative feedback from the feedback summary, then you will need to discuss this with him and possibly find a replacement. Just because he's getting things closed doesn't mean he's making your clients happy or giving them what I call the "warm fuzzy feeling."

Likewise, if you receive a lot of positive feedback for "Bob the Mortgage Broker," this will confirm that you've made a good decision in having him on your team.

Happy clients refer and tell others how great the experience was. Unhappy clients don't refer, but they do tell others how the experience was for them.

Another part of this form is asking the buyer/seller to provide testimonials about the service. As you build your business, it's helpful to have supporting evidence for future prospects about the level of satisfaction others have had in working with you and your team.

The final portion of the feedback summary forms is asking the buyer/seller to provide you with a list of anyone who is considering buying or selling a home. Ask them to complete the individual's name and contact info so you can contact them.

Some buyers/sellers may not want to provide you with contact information for others and will say something like "let me tell them about you and give them your information." Here is the way I suggest you counter this one: "I see your position on this, and generally don't like my information shared, but if one of my friends knows that I could really benefit from a service and should learn more about it, I'm grateful to them for their help. I know you're going to be busy with moving and I wouldn't want your friend to miss an opportunity while you're busy." While this one doesn't always work, if you believe it, and you feel confident in your sales ability, you'll get the info most of the time.

A better way to gather testimonials is to have a video camera to capture the voice and image of the person giving the testimonial. Almost any smart phone will take a good video that you can then add to your website and other marketing channels.

Here's my point with this one: how many times have you read a testimonial online or in an advertisement that simply said "Larry W., Florida" and thought to yourself, *really*?!?!?' I'm sure often, and this is why getting the testimonial recorded lends additional credibility to you and your business.

You have to "strike while the iron is hot," and have the tools to get the recording. If you rely on them to call a number to leave a recorded testimonial or send you a video later, the chances of you getting this go way down.

If you're planning to attend closing you can capture their testimonial right there in the conference room after everything is finalized.

Word of caution: *Remind the ladies you'll be doing this, trust me; at the top of my list of annoying things is someone who takes a photo or video of me when my hair is un-coifed or I haven't put on any makeup. You* *won't get a testimonial from me no matter how much you beg if I'm not feeling good. I am sure I also represent many of my fellow ladies in this.*

Several of my investor clients have used the suggestion of having their favorite title company handle this for them, which is especially helpful when they are not able to attend closing. Simply buy an inexpensive video camera and ask the title company to keep it in a safe place for all your closings. Give them detailed instructions as well as samples on the type of testimonial you're looking for.

If the client won't do video because they are camera-shy, you could offer them the option to record a voice testimonial. Again, this is a feature available on most smart phones. Alternatively, you could have the client call and leave a voice message. Google Voice would be a great option for this, as the recording is then a .wav or .mp3 file.

Once you have these testimonials and, of course, permission to use them, add them to your website, printed marketing materials, and other presentation materials, as well as using the Internet to post them online in places like YouTube.com and Facebook. In addition to providing credibility about your services, with the right key words, these videos will drive traffic to your website.

Success stories are a favorite of mine at TMC. Several times a year I schedule interviews with my clients. I send them a few questions, then we meet on a conference line and I record the call. Generally it involves no editing, and it's quickly available for me to download, then add to our website. You can hear success stories from many of our Realtor and investor clients by going to www.TransactionManagementConsultants.com and clicking on the success stories tab.

You've got your testimonial, you've received your commission check, it's time to check your documents, tidy up the file and keep everything needed in a safe place.

I highly recommend you do this digitally. Simply scan the items, put them onto your computer, and save a copy if you'd like on Google Drive, formerly known as Google Docs. You may want to consider sharing the file with your client, so if they want to access any of the docs in the future they could simply go the file and pick up what they need.

What to keep in your files after closing

(Laws may vary in your state, this is only a guideline.)

o **Contract and Addenda** – While closing completes the contract, it's still advisable, and, in most states required by the real estate governing body, that you maintain a copy of it and all addenda. If a question occurs about fees, personal property conveyed, etc. having this to refer back to is critical.

o **Disclosures** – If real property disclosures were part of your transaction, you should maintain a copy of them.

o **Correspondence** – Maintaining a good communication log during the transaction will make this simple. I also suggest you file all written correspondence including key emails.

o **Final executed HUD or closing statement** – At closing, you and the buyer/seller will review and sign a closing statement. You should keep a copy for many reasons. Here are several: 1) Taxes; your accountant or CPA will need this to complete your taxes correctly. 2) Possible future questions about the transaction and items paid. 3) Realtors you should send a copy to your client in January of the year after their closing. This is a great help to them in getting what they need together to file their taxes. More than once I've heard stories of Realtors who do this and receive referrals for this little act.

- o **Repair Receipts** – Any work done should be documented. Copies of receipts for work should also be shared with the buyer. If there is an issue later with, say, the roof you had repaired, the buyer can access their copy. Alternatively, if they should call you, you'll have a copy in your records to provide them so that they can contact the roofer who made the repairs for additional support.

- o **Testimonials** – I've already discussed getting them, here you'll want to keep a copy and also a copy of the agreement or authorization for you to use them.

I've always been of the school of thought in real estate transactions and documentation that *"when in doubt, KEEP IT."* You never know when an item you've tossed will be needed. Now that all of these items can be kept digitally, it's really no extra work or storage space to keep a few extra papers.

When I started out in real estate as a sales agent, I had large files when my deals were done and maintained a copy in my home office as well as in my broker's office. Over the years I discovered that scanning these items and keeping them was far easier and also has helped me immensely when moving my office several times. It also gave one of my children an opportunity to earn some extra money by scanning everything for me and eliminated the need for me to do it.

If you've managed your deals by paper, taking the time to scan them and save them in a few folders on your computer, then back up as suggested via Google Drive. This will make them easily accessible later should you need to review or use any of the documents.

Thankfully most everything is digital in today's modern real estate transactions.

Here is how I suggest you set this up:

Create a folder with address for property (123 Main Street)

- Communication – emails, notes and communication log
- Contract and addenda – executed copies
- Title docs – include survey, title insurance
- Repair receipts
- Testimonials and feedback summary(s)
- Misc – everything else

Once you've scanned in your documents, verified they scanned properly, and backed up the data, unless your state requires you to keep paper, you can freely destroy the paper file.

If any of the technology of scanning or uploading videos feels daunting or overwhelming don't fret about it. I'm a big fan of delegating and in a subsequent chapter I'll share with you ways to have much of the busy work in your business or the things that you're not good at done by others.

"Small deeds done are better than great deeds planned." Peter Marshall

"One reason so few of us achieve what we truly want is that we never direct our focus; we never concentrate our power. Most people dabble their way through life, never deciding to master anything in particular." Tony Robbins

Chapter 10

EFFECTIVE TIME MANAGEMENT

We all have the same 24 hours in a day; it's how we use them that either bring us closer to our goals or takes us away from them. It's up to us to choose wisely how we spend our time.

If there is one thing I've learned is that we all have the power to control how our time is used, and we always make time for the things that are really important to us or that we really need.

For instance, when I run out of coffee or half-n-half, I always make time to go to the store. We could be out of lettuce or bread, and we could make due with other items on hand for a meal or snack, but there is no way I am skipping my morning coffee.

Same is true with physical exercise. For me walking is my favorite; I enjoy spending time walking on the intercostal bridge by my house or at the beach just a few blocks away. This wasn't always the case, I would often wake up, have coffee and go straight upstairs to my office where it always seemed like there was something to do. Then I realized that if I wanted to change my physical appearance and have more energy I needed to lace up my sneakers, put on my shades, and hit the pavement. I now use this time to listen to audio programs so I'm learning as I walk.

Another lesson on time that I've learned is that we have a tendency to fill up what we have. In other words if I say to myself I'm going to work in my office from 9am to 5pm, stopping for lunch somewhere along the way, I will fill up that time with activity and some may carry over till tomorrow, after all much of my writing and business planning doesn't generally have deadlines unless I impose them on myself. Yet when I am leaving for a conference or a vacation and I need to accomplish things before I leave I can get an amazing amount of work done in a shorter period of time. I'm not alone; we've all witnessed this first hand and it's the deadline we've imposed, the "we can't do this tomorrow because we'll be on a plane" mindset that forces us to focus. While I don't work like this daily I am working on doing this more often than not. In Tim Ferris' book *The Four Hour Work Week,* another excellent read on time management and delegating he talks about this idea.

Think about that next time you sit at your desk, give yourself a goal, say writing a blog post in the next 30 minutes, then turn off all distractions, light a candle (that's how I do it), and write. I bet you can easily get 600 words of great significance on a page in 30 minutes if you focus.

Then try this with another task and another and before you know it *BAM*, you're getting more stuff done in less time, meaning you can have more play time and more time to grow your business.

Recently I read, or actually reread, a great book by Dan Kennedy called the *No B.S. Time Management for Entrepreneurs, The Ultimate No Holds Barred, Kick Butt, Take No Prisoners Guide to Time Productivity & Sanity.*

It's a sort of in your face, no holds barred, book about time management. I've found many of the ideas helpful in my businesses and am sharing with you some which I've implemented into my business in the hope that they will inspire you to use your work time with sincerity and focus.

Know the value of your time and pay yourself first. Establish what you expect to make income wise, then figure out the per hour rate that you'll need to generate to reach that income. Remember of course that even the best don't get in a full eight hours of productive work each day. *Many of us have no desire to put in a full eight hours of work either, we'd rather work six and then play more*. Determine how many hours you aren't productive at making income; i.e. driving to appointments, filing documents, faxing, time on hold, chit chatting, day dreaming, wandering around on the Internet, playing on social media, etc. and subtract them from the equation.

In other words, if you plan to make $150k per year, then the formula for determining your hourly rate would look something like this.

> At 40 hours per week and 52 hours in a year, there are 2080 hours to work. Of those 80 should be vacation and 40 for personal and sick days.

> This leaves us 1960 working hours. Now, here's where the real formula for making us think about the value of our time. How productive are we during those 1960 working hours? This will determine our hourly rate. There is no one, at least human, that can work at 100% productivity all the time; no matter how focused you are, you're also human. So you'll have to figure out how productive you are in your day, but for this example let's say 60% productive. Based on that the number of hours worked are 1176 and to make the income goal of $150k, you'll need to pay yourself $127.55 per hour. Let's take this one step further, if you're only able to work at 50% productivity, then the number of hours worked is 980 per year and you'll need to pay yourself $153.06 per hour to hit your income goal of $150k.

Next time you pick up the phone, walk to the copier or any other activity, stop and ask yourself, is this something I'd pay someone else $150.00 an hour (or whatever your number is) to do? Or is this an activity I need to delegate or eliminate?

*Knowing what our time is worth is a
real awakening for most of us.*

Minimize interruptions. In Dan's book he calls people who steal your time "Time Vampires." I love the way he puts it, and when you really think about it, he's right. He explains that just minutes interrupted in your day can lead to fewer and fewer productive hours over the course of a week, month, and year. Many of the ideas in this book—specifically the checklists and delegating the follow-up to a transaction coordinator or an administrative assistant—are designed to help you minimize your interruptions by having others get you updates, not you chasing them down.

Dan writes if we want to really manage our time, it's our job to slay the "Time Vampires" and regain control. Some examples are the people who just wander by your office and stop by with a quick question or thought.

This is why using the transaction coordinator who is in your brokerage may not be ideal, and the one that works virtually is likely to be able to get more done for you in a shorter period of time. While to many they may seem harmless, in fact they are dangerous.

These people, while they may not intend it, really have no value for your time. They feel that their little interruption is more important that whatever you were doing. The best way to control them is to be busy, shut your door and turn off your phone. But if they persist, you must drive a stake right through their heart (his words, not mine) and take the upper hand. When they stop by unannounced, say something like "I'm really busy working on a deadline right now, let's talk at four."

You can do this with people who call you, as well. It may take a few "stakes" to get their attention and regain control of your time, but trust me, it's so worth it.

My other favorite suggestion is that when you begin a conversation with someone, let them know how much time they have and stick to it. "Hi, Sally, I'm really pressed for time, but I also want to help you. I only have about ten minutes, so we'll need to get right to the point." Amazingly, this one also works very well.

Taking a few actions each day to reduce or eliminate the interruptions can lead to hours each week and thousands of dollars each year.

Turn time into wealth. Think about the unproductive time you have in the day, driving, standing in line, waiting on an appointment, etc. Then find ways to turn that time into something other than the clock simply ticking by. Always carry a book with you. I read about a book every week to two weeks, depending on my schedule and the thickness of the book. Ever since my kids were old enough to flip the pages of a book they also were taught to take a book with them when we got in the car. I can't begin to tell you how much this has improved my life. Finding time to read at night or maybe during the day when others are around can be difficult. But when I'm waiting at an appointment, I can fill in that time with productive activities and read something new.

Dan also suggests taking CDs with you to listen to them while you drive around town. I've taken this one step further and listen to audio programs while I walk and sometimes when I'm alone in the kitchen cooking or cleaning. My collection is vast of the CDs I've listened to and learned from. Many I've even listened to several times over. Now with the MP3 world, it's even easier to buy audio books, download them to your MP3 player and take that with you everywhere. Many cars even have a jack to plug one into. If you commute for work, imagine how many hours of education you can have at the end of the year.

You'll have time to learn a new language, new business strategies, personal growth lessons, and so much more. It's up to you how you use your time and *yes*, I also do enjoy my 80's channel in the car, especially when the weather is nice and the top is down.

All in all it's really up to us to determine the thing or things that are the most important to generating income in our business. I'm just as guilty as the next guy of checking my smart phone way too often, replying instantly to something that could have waited until I finished lunch. Or getting to work with only a list of things to do, nothing on the calendar to say from 12:00 to 1:00 write blog, and from 2:00 to 2:30 check email, etc.

Too often we just show up, the day happens and at the end we can't figure out why we aren't getting more from our business. What I really aspire to, and suggest you do also, is to be in control of our time. With a few tweaks in the way things are done, little by little, you'll see it really change for you, having more time to do the activities that make the phone ring and generate sales.

Lastly on time management, **schedule the important things now**. Things like vacations, days off, birthday celebrations, anniversary dinners, etc. What we don't commit to our schedule we often will not do. So pull out your calendar or log into it online, check with the family and figure out where you'd like to go and when for vacation then *put* it on the calendar.

"The key is not to prioritize what's on your schedule, but to schedule your priorities." Stephen Covey

"If you think you can do it alone, you're thinking too small." Nancy Solomon

Chapter 11

WORKING WITH A VIRTUAL TRANSACTION COORDINATOR OR A VIRTUAL ASSISTANT

Before I go into how having a virtual assistant can help you in your real estate business or where to find one, I want to discuss time management and delegating. While it may sound sexy to have an assistant, or exotic to have one from another country, if you're doing it "just because everyone else is," then it's not for the reasons that will help you build a successful business.

What is the number one activity that generates income for your business?

Is it faxing, calling to schedule closing appointments, coordinating appointments for home inspection, filing contracts in your office? *No*. You and I both know the answer is a resounding *no*. But yet, many of us continue to do it. A broker I was speaking with recently told me he says to the agents in his office "you don't want to be the highest paid person at the copy machine."

There are many schools of thoughts on delegating and why people don't. Over the years I've chatted with many people about this subject. Some tell me that it takes too long to find and train someone and they can do it better. I say, *false*! Some explain that they've tried in the past to delegate, but the person or people that they hired, "just didn't work out." Mmmmmm—who chose who? Others claim that the costs prohibit them from bringing someone into the business and that when their business improves, they plan to start looking for someone. Okay, maybe, but if you always do it all, how can you do more? There are only so many hours in the day.

AGGH!!!! Why do so many real estate agents think they have to do it all, or are supposed to? And, honestly, many people are still teaching that you can do it all, be it all, and have it all? Do they really expect us to believe that top producers are licking envelopes, creating brochures or calling to see what time a closing is scheduled for? *No, no, no,* of course they aren't. If you're serious about building a successful business, that provides you income and free time, then you've got to stop licking envelopes and doing other activities like that and start delegating.

Without a doubt, I can tell you that once I started doing this, my life and my business truly changed.

In the last chapter I stated my case on time management and how having someone or *many some ones* help you is the only true way to build a business that works for you, not the other way around. The next question everyone asks is "where do I find one?" "How can I bring someone into my business that I've never met, or have them do things for me that I don't even understand?" It's really easier than you may think. First let's define what a virtual assistant is:

> *According to Wikipedia* - *A Virtual Assistant (or simply, "VA") is an independent contractor providing administrative, technical, or sometimes creative assistance to clients — usually to other independent entrepreneurs and solo and small business practices, such as that of a lawyer or realtor. Virtual assistants work from their own office (hence "virtual"),*

thus making it a fairly popular (and growing) profession.

There is a lot of buzz online and in the papers about outsourcing. There are many websites that function as meeting places to help the businessperson find help, and also to protect each other. Most of these sites will allow you to post a job opening at no cost. Then you interview candidates until you find one that meets your expectations. Once you've selected the individual who you feel will do the best work for you, you send them work and generally wait for them to email you that the work is done and request new assignments. Many entrepreneurs, especially what we call solo-preneuers, use these types of assistants to achieve maximum results with minimum expense.

For example, there is generally no reason to hire a bookkeeper full-time in your small real estate business if you don't have forty hours' worth of bookkeeping work a week. If you hire a virtual bookkeeper, and give her five hours of work a week, she has thirty-five hours left to service other clients and you're only paying for a fraction of her salary. ***Genius, right?***

There are many things you could have a virtual assistant handle, for some things on your to do list may never get done if you don't get help. Here's a brief list to give you some ideas to help you get your delegating muscle working:

- ☐ Research

- ☐ Data entry

- ☐ Updating or redoing your website

- ☐ Video editing

- ☐ Uploading videos

- ☐ Editing articles and blog posts

- ☐ Graphics/flyers/brochures

- ☐ Social media

- ☐ Email marketing

- ☐ Maintaining and updating your CRM

With a little creativity, some great instructions, and clear expectations, you can have someone handle many items in your business that are taking up too much of your valuable time,

"If you can dream it, you can do it." Walt Disney

For any control freaks let me say that — contrary to popular belief — *being in control isn't about doing it all, being in control is about getting things done, consistently and correctly*. With only twenty-four hours in a day, if we don't leverage ourselves, we may never reach our goals, or if we do, when we get there, we'll likely be too worn out to enjoy it.

Finding the right person to help you may take a while and really is not unlike hiring someone to work in your office. If you've ever had the opportunity to do the hiring for yourself or someplace you've worked before, you understand that this can be a challenge.

If you're interested in hiring a virtual assistant who can help you with your real estate marketing, I've provided you information on trusted and highly skilled team in the resources section of this book.

Making a case for hiring a virtual transaction coordinator

Agent myth: My clients (buyers, sellers, investors, etc.) will only work with me—only I can deliver quality service.

Fact: They aren't loyal to you; they are loyal to the standards you represent. Making sure they get what they want, a closed deal, with little to no hassle is what they truly want. You and *your team* can do this and you'll work far less by hiring a transaction coordinator to assist you.

Agent myth: No one can do it the way I like it done or the way I do it.

Fact: *Wrong*—anyone can provide great service to your buyer/seller from contract to close and they *can* do it your way if you provide them with the training, tools, and resources to get the job done.

Agent myth: It's too expensive to have help; maybe one day when my business grows I'll be able to afford to hire someone.

Fact: Just delegating a few things here and there will help you train your mind to look at your business differently. Perhaps you hire someone to create flyers, enter your new listings onto the various sites that you use to market them to, or you have a transaction coordinator handle your new contract. In all of these scenarios you are only paying for the project, not for that person to work a certain number of hours. It doesn't get much easier or more cost effective than that to bring someone on to help you leverage your time so you can grow your business.

What exactly is a transaction coordinator? It is the person who takes responsibility for getting a contract to the closing table. If you don't have someone in your office or on your team helping you, you're the coordinator! Hiring someone to assist in managing a transaction from contract through closing is an incredible way to free up your time to give you more time to focus on putting more deals together. When you're ready to start delegating and even outsourcing to a coordinator, here's a brief description of their job.

☐ Processing of the contract through closing. The coordinator is in charge of moving the paper around, making sure everyone has a copy of the contract, addenda and disclosures. They are also responsible for ensuring that the doc are complete. All the signatures, dates and required initials are in their respective places. If the document is missing something, they should bring it to your attention and have it corrected.

☐ Communicating with all parties, getting updates for you, answering questions where possible, scheduling appointments, following up on requests and documents, etc.

☐ Tracking the contract deadlines and seeing to it that they are adhered to. This means staying on top of the items that have been agreed upon by the buyer and seller in the contract, making sure that they are met and contacting you or the agent/real estate investor if one will not be.

☐ Coordinating appointments for inspections, appraisals and closing. It can take sometimes ten calls or more to coordinate everyone's schedules to secure a home inspection appointment. These calls can and should be made by your coordinator. Your coordinator will not only make sure that these are scheduled, but track the results and circulate any necessary reports to the appropriate parties.

☐ Effectively communicates with clients, customers, other agents, lenders, title agents and other service providers throughout the process. Having all the details in front of him/her will make handling the inquiries much easier. If you're taking calls and don't have all the details in front of you, it's hard to do your job effectively.

☐ Responsible for proper documentation of the file to comply with office and state policies. Your transaction coordinator will have a checklist of the items you want in your files.

They will make sure those documents are
collected for your file and shared with the
appropriate parties.

☐   Assures that all post-closing disbursements,
filing, and procedures take place. Being on top
of it all, managing and even nagging when
needed is what it takes to get the job done.
Seeing that everything comes together means
that everyone gets paid.

☐   Post-closing follow-up. Your coordinator will
make sure that all of the closing docs you
wanted in the file are collected. Some may also
gather testimonials, feedback, and referrals.
Lastly, they will double check the file for
accuracy before "archiving" it.

Some real estate offices have a coordinator on staff that is
shared among the office. Those coordinators are made
available for the agents to build their business. If you are not
part of an office that offers one, or the one in your office is too
busy and/or doesn't meet your expectations, hire a virtual
closing coordinator. It's truly not cost effective to hire a
coordinator to work exclusively for you in most situations and
sit in your office (see the salary break down below).
Additionally, there really is no need either if you tap into the
power of virtual outsourcing. If you're interested in hiring a
virtual transaction coordinator, I've provided you information
on locating on in the resources section of this book.

Typical Costs of a Full Time Transaction Coordinator

Typical Salary	$36,000/ $17.31/hr.
Paid Vacation	$1385
Temp during Vacation	$2000
Health Insurance (employer portion 12 mos.@$200)	$2400
FICA Taxes (7.65%)	$2754
Worker's Comp. (.61%)	$220
Unemployment (State & Fed)	$309
Misc. costs (Vision, Dental, Disability & 401K Matching, Profit Sharing & Stock Options)	$???
Office Space for TC 100 s.f. @ applicable rate	$2500 $25/s.f. is conservative
Cost of Overtime Pay (10hrs/ mo @ 50% premium)	$3115
Idle time during employer's absence (min. 2 wk vacation included for employer)	$1500
Annual Bonus (1 mo. salary)	$3000
Sick Time (10 days/year)	$1385
Other intangible costs (furniture, testing, training & fees, sick children, etc.)	$1200 Conservative figure
Total Typical All In Costs	$57,768/ $27.77/hr. 1.60 times salary
Total Effective hourly rate	$27.77/hour
75% Productive Level	$37.03/hour
50% Productive Level	$55.55/hour

A virtual assistant can help you with other activities in your business, not just coordinating your transactions. I routinely teach a course called "Building a Virtual Dream Team" where I walk participants through the steps I've mastered that have allowed me to have an entire team of people working for me from locations all over the US and many other parts of the world. The same ones I've used to help my coaching and consulting clients create virtual dream teams for their businesses. In the resources section of this book you'll find details on where you can learn about taking one of these workshops.

If you can't wait for a workshop, you can pick up copy of the book I wrote on the topic called "Do What You Love; Delegate The Rest" you'll find it on Amazon under that title or my name.

I'm a big fan of going virtual and it's one that has allowed me to have the freedom and flexibility I wanted when I started my business back in 2005.

You don't have to do it alone and if you try, you'll never reach your goals; surround yourself little by little with a team that can help you reach your big dreams.

If you're the only one doing everything in your business, then you are on a fast track for a breakdown.

"It has been my observation that most people get ahead during the time that others waste." Henry Ford

Chapter 12

GLOSSARY OF REAL ESTATE TERMS

Every industry has its own language and in real estate there are plenty of words or phrases that you don't find in any other business. I've done my best to compile a list of the ones that you will most likely come across at one time or another as well as provide a description that is easy to understand. Keep this handy as a reference to save you time when something comes up in the future.

Abstract of Title (Abstract) – The condensed history of a parcel of real estate, compiled from public records, listing transfers of ownership, claims against the property and certified by the abstractor that the history is complete.

Addendum – An addition to the sales contract.

Acceleration Clause – A provision or clause in a mortgage document stating that if a payment is missed or any other provision of the mortgage is violated, the whole debt becomes immediately due and payable.

Acknowledgment – The formal declaration before a public official (Notary) that one has signed a document.

Acre – Land measure equal to 43,560 square feet.

Adjustable-Rate Mortgage (ARM) – Loan whose interest rate is changed periodically by the lender according to its governing index.

Adjusted Basis – The original cost of a property plus any later improvements and minus a figure for depreciation claimed

Adjusted Sales Price - Sale price minus commissions, legal fees, and other costs of selling.

Adjustment Date – The day which an adjustment is made to an adjustable rate mortgage. This may occur monthly, annually, or as otherwise agreed.

Agent – Person authorized to act on behalf of another in dealing with third parties.

Agency – One who acts or has the power to act for another.

Agreement of Sale (purchase agreement, sales agreement, contract to purchase) – The written contract detailing terms under which the buyer agrees to buy and the seller agrees to sell.

Alienation Clause (*due-on-sale, non-assumption*) – A provision or clause in a mortgage document stating that the loan must be paid in full if ownership is transferred; sometimes contingent upon other occurrences.

Amenities – The special features of a home, development, or condominium community.

American Land Title Association (ALTA) – A more complete and extensive policy of title insurance which most lenders require, it often guarantees the property's boundaries.

Amortization – The process of repayment of a loan gradually through regular installments that cover both principal and interest.

Annual Percentage Rate (APR) – The actual interest rate paid on a loan, including interest, loan fees, and points. The

APR is determined by a government formula and generally disclosed on the Truth in Lending Disclosure Statement, often called the TIL.

Appraisal – The process of determining the estimate of value of real estate, presumably by an expert. Also, the report which sets forth the value is often called the appraisal or appraisal report.

Appreciation – Increase in value or worth of property.

As-Is – The sale of a property sold with no warrantees by the seller in the present condition. This does not absolve them of the responsibility of making disclosures as to the condition of the property.

Assessed Valuation – Value placed on property as a basis for levying property taxes, not identical with appraised or market value.

Assignment – Transfer of a contract from one party to another.

Assignment of Mortgage – The lender's sale of a mortgage which does not generally require a borrower's permission.

Assumable Mortgage – A loan that may be passed to the next owner of the property and generally requires qualification by the lender.

Assumption – The taking over of a loan by any qualified buyer.

Automatic Renewal Clause – A clause or provision that allows a listing contract to be renewed indefinitely unless canceled by the property owner.

Back-end Ratio – The ratio, or percentage, that the lender uses to compare a borrower's total debt (PITI plus other monthly debt payments, i.e. car loans or credit cards) to gross monthly income.

Back-up Offer – A secondary bid for a property that the seller agrees to accept if the first offer from a different buyer fails.

Balance (home/life/work) – A *fairy tale*; life is full of things that pull us. Keep focused on what you want, make the best of the situations as they come up and *get help* when you can.

Balloon Loan – Mortgage in which the remaining balance becomes fully dead and payable at a predetermined time.

Balloon Payment – A single final payment on a balloon loan that is larger than all the other payments.

Bill of Sale – Written document transferring personal property.

Binder – Preliminary agreement of sale, usually accompanied by earnest money. (Term also used with property insurance.)

Biweekly Mortgage – A mortgage that is paid every other week instead of monthly, resulting in the equivalent of one month's extra payment per year.

Blanket Mortgage – A mortgage that covers several properties instead of a single property. This type of mortgage is used most frequently by developers and builders.

Broker – Person licensed by the state to represent another for a fee in real estate transactions.

Built-Ins – Appliances, cabinetry, or fixtures that are attached to a home. These built-ins cannot easily be removed and are considered part of the sale. Often referred to as glued and screwed.

Building Code – Regulations of local government stipulating requirements and standards for building and construction.

Bummer – When you've worked hard to put a deal together, and for reasons beyond your control it doesn't make it to the closing table.

Buydown Mortgage – The payment of additional points to a mortgage lender in return for a lower than market rate on a loan, either for the entire term or a set period at the beginning.

Buyer's Broker or Buyer's Agent – A real estate agent who takes the buyer as a client, is obligated to put the buyer's interests above all others, and owes specific fiduciary duties to the buyer.

Buyer's Market – Situation in which supply of homes for sale exceeds demand; often called a slow market.

Cancellation Clause – Sometimes called the "liquidated damages" in a purchase agreement, the clause that details the conditions under which either buyer or seller may terminate the contract.

Cap – A limit which an adjustable mortgage rate might be raised at any one time.

Capital Gain – Taxable profit on the sale of an appreciated asset.

Caveat Emptor – Let the buyer beware.

Ceiling – Also known as lifetime cap; limit beyond which an adjustable mortgage rate may never be raised.

Certificate of Occupancy – A document issued by local governmental agencies stating that property meets standards for occupancy.

Chain of Title – The history of ownership of a property. The title to the property forms a chain going back to the first owners. Lenders often require a chain of title report going back only several years.

Chattel – Personal property.

Closing (may also be called settlement or escrow) – A meeting to conclude the real estate sale, at which time title is transferred and funds change hands.

Closing Costs – One-time charges paid buy buyer and seller on the day property changes hands.

Closing Statement (HUD-1 Settlement Statement) – A detailed cash accounting of a real estate transaction between the buyer and seller listing debits and credits, completed by the person in charge of the closing.

Cloud on Title – Outstanding claims or encumbrance that challenges the owner's clear title.

Commission – The fee paid for broker's services in securing a buyer for a property, usually a percentage of sales price and generally paid by the seller.

Commitment (letter) – A written promise to grant a mortgage loan to a borrower.

Common Elements – Parts of a condominium development in which each owner holds an interest.

Comparables (Comps) – Properties used in an appraisal or other market analysis which are substantially equivalent to the subject property. These are used to estimate market value of the subject property.

Comparative Market Analysis – A comparison of the prices of homes recently sold and current homes similar to the seller's home. This is used to determine a listing price of a home and is generally prepared by a real estate agent.

Conditional Commitment – Lender's promise to make a loan subject to the fulfillment of specified conditions.

Conditional Offer – Purchase offer in which buyer promises to purchase only after certain occurrences. (i.e., sale of another home, securing of financing, home inspections, etc.)

Condominium – A type of ownership in involving individual ownership of a dwelling unit (interior space) and common ownership of shared areas such as pools, parking lots, tennis courts, or other common areas.

Conforming Loan – A mortgage that complies fully with the underwriting requirements of Fannie Mae or Freddie Mac.

Consideration – Anything of value given to induce another to enter into a contract.

Contingency – A condition that must be satisfied before the buyer purchases a home. I.e., satisfactory home inspection, obtaining a mortgage, selling existing residence.

Contract – A legally enforceable agreement to do a particular thing for which, if breached, the law provides a remedy.

Contract for Deed – Also called a land contract; it's a method of selling whereby the buyer receives possession of the property, but the seller retains title.

Conventional Loan (Conventional Mortgage) – A loan arranged between lender and buyer with no governmental guarantee or insurance.

Convertible Mortgage – An adjustable rate mortgage with a provision or clause allowing it to be converted to a fixed rate mortgage at some time in the future.

Cosigner – Someone with better credit – generally a close relative – who agrees to sign your loan if by yourself you do not qualify for a mortgage. They generally are equally responsible for the repayment of the loan.

Cost Basis – Accounting figure that includes original cost of property plus certain expenses to purchase, money spent on permanent improvements and other costs, minus depreciation claimed on tax returns over the years.

Covenants, Conditions, and Restrictions (CC&Rs) – Limits on the types of activities you, as a property owner, may engage in on the property.

Counteroffer – A response to an offer that may contain changes to the original offer. There is no legally binding contract until the buyer and seller are in agreement to all terms, in writing.

Credit – (in relation to a closing transaction) Reflected on a closing statement or HUD-1 Settlement Statement as an amount entered in a person's favor—either an amount the party has paid in advance, i.e. escrow deposit, or an amount which the party is being reimbursed for, i.e. needed repairs.

Credit Report – An official report from the credit bureaus which shows an applicant's history of payments made to other or previous creditors.

Days on the Market (DOM) – The number of days between the time a house is put on the market and the date of a firm sale contract.

Debit – (in relation to a closing transaction) Reflected on a closing statement or HUD-1 Settlement Statement as an amount entered in a charged; i.e. settlement fee, taxes, loan costs.

Deed – The formal written document transferring title to real estate; a new deed is used for each transfer.

Deed of Trust – A document by which title to property is held by a neutral third party until a debt is paid; used instead of a mortgage in some states. It gives a lender the right to foreclose on a property if the borrower defaults on the loan.

Deed Restrictions (restrictive covenant) – Provision placed in a deed to control use and occupancy of the property's future owners.

Default – Failure to make mortgage payment.

Deferred Maintenance – The needed repairs that have been put off.

Deficiency Judgment – A personal claim against the debtor when foreclosed property does not yield enough at sale to pay off loans against it.

Delivery – The legal transfer of a deed to the new property owner, the moment at which transfer of title occurs.

Deposit – The money the buyer puts up also called earnest money, to demonstrate their seriousness in making an offer. The deposit is usually at risk if the buyer fails to complete the transaction and has no contractual way of backing out of the deal.

Depreciation – Decrease in value of property because of deterioration or obsolescence; sometimes, an artificial bookkeeping concept which is valuable as a tax shelter.

Discount Point – A unit of measurement used for various loan charges; one point equals one percent of the amount of the loan.

Documentary Stamps/Transfer Tax – A charge levied by

state or local governments when real estate is transferred or mortgaged. Generally paid by the seller when the deed is recorded.

Down Payment – Cash to be paid by the buyer at closing.

Dual Agency or Dual Agent – An agent representing both buyer and seller in a transaction. In many states it's illegal, and in others there must be consent by both buyer and seller to act as a dual agent.

Due-on-Sale Clause – A clause or provision in a mortgage which states that the entire unpaid balance becomes due and payable upon the sale of the property.

DVA – Department of Veterans Affairs; formerly VA, Veterans Administration.

Earnest Money – Buyer's "good faith" deposit accompanying purchase offer.

Easement – A permanent right to use another's property.

Encroachment – Unauthorized intrusion of a building or improvement into another's land.

Encumbrance – A right or claim against another's real estate, i.e. a mortgage, tax, or judgment lien. An easement or restriction on the use of the land is also an encumbrance.

Equity – The money realized when property is sold and all the claims against it are paid. Commonly sales price minus present mortgage and closing costs.

Escrow – Funds given to a third party to be held pending some occurrence, may refer to earnest money, funds collected by lender for the payment of taxes and insurance charges; funds withheld at closing to insure uncompleted repairs'. In some states the entire closing process is referred to as escrow.

Escrow Company – An independent third party that handles funds, carries out the instructions of the lender, buyer, and seller in the transaction, and handles all the documents.

Exclusive Listing Agency – Listing agreement under which only the listing office can sell the property and keep the commission, except if the owner sells the house, in which case no commission is paid.

Exclusive Right of Sell – A type of listing agreement under which the owner promises to pay a commission if the property is sold during the listing period by anyone, even the owner.

Facilitator – One who offers real estate services without owning special fiduciary duties to either buyer or seller.

Fair Housing Act – A federal law which prohibits discrimination of any individual based on race, color, religion, sex, handicap, marital status and national origin.

Fairy Godmother – An enchanting and skilled *fairy* who can help one see things clearly and in a way that will help them get the results they want. Fairy Godmothers can appear in person or virtually. Learn more at www.VirtualFairyGodmother.com

FHA – The Federal Housing Administration (HUD), which insures mortgages to protect the lending institution in case of default.

Fannie Mae – Formerly called the Federal National Mortgage Association, it is a publicly held company that buys mortgages from lenders and resells them as securities on the secondary mortgage market.

FHA Loan or FHA Mortgage – A loan which is insured by the Federal Housing Authority and made by a local lending institution, with the borrower paying an insurance premium, usually upfront at closing.

Fee Simple – Highest possible degree of ownership of land.

Fiduciary – A person in a position of trust or responsibility with specific duties to act in the best interest of the client.

First Mortgage – The primary mortgage holding priority over the claims of subsequent lenders against the same property.

Fixed-rate Mortgage – A home loan with an interest rate that will remain at the same specific rate for the term of the loan.

Fixture – Personal property that has become part of the real estate.

Foreclosure – The legal procedure a lender must take to enforce payment of debt by seizing and selling the mortgaged property.

Freddie Mac – A publicly traded security collateralized by a pool of mortgages backed by the Federal Home Loan Mortgage Corporation, a secondary lender.

FSBO (For Sale By Owner) – A property for sale, but where the owner has chosen not to work with an outside agent, broker, or other representation.

Garbage Fees or Junk Fees – Extra and often unwarranted charges tacked on when a buyer obtains a mortgage.

Good Faith Estimate – An estimate that the lender must provide, by law, to a prospective borrower which shows the costs the borrower will incur for obtaining a loan with this lender.

Graduated-Payment Mortgage – A mortgage where payments vary over the life of the loan. The payments generally start out low, then slowly rise until they reach a plateau where they will remain for the balance of a loan.

Grantee – The buyer, who receives a deed

Grantor – The seller, who gives a deed.

Grumpy Buyer – The person least likely to give you a referral after they move into their home.

Guaranteed Sale – A promise by the listing broker that if the property cannot be sold by a specific date, the broker will buy it, usually at a sharply discounted price.

Hazard Insurance – Insurance on a property against fire and similar risks.

Homeowners Association (HOA) – A group that sets and enforces rules in a condominium, town house, or other planned community of single family homes.

Homeowners Policy – A standardized package of insurance that puts many kinds of insurance together into one policy.

Home Warranty – A type of insurance that covers repairs to certain parts of a home and some fixtures after a buyer moves in. The premium for this type of coverage is paid at closing and generally for a one year coverage. Most warranty companies do offer renewal opportunities for homeowners after the initial term.

Improvements – Permanent additions that increase the value of a home.

Index – A measurement of an established interest rate, used to determine the periodic adjustments for an adjustable rate mortgage.

Inspection Report – A report, usually prepared by a professional inspector and obtained by the buyer which summarizes the condition of the home's various components.

Joint Tenancy – Ownership by two or more persons, each with an undivided ownership – if one dies, the property automatically goes to the survivor.

Jumbo Loan – A loan that exceeds the limits set by Fannie Mae and Freddie Mac, making it a nonconforming loan.

Junior Mortgage – A mortgage subordinate to another, also referred to as a second or third mortgage.

Lien – A claim against property for the payment of a debt; mechanic's lien, mortgage, unpaid taxes, judgments.

Lis Pendens – Notice that litigation is pending on a property.

Listing Agreement – A written contract or employment agreement between a property owner (seller) and a real estate broker, authorizing the broker to find a buyer.

Listing Presentation – Proposal submitted by a real estate agent who seeks to put a prospective seller's property on the market.

Loan Servicing – Handling paperwork of collecting loan payments, checking property tax and insurance coverage, handling delinquencies.

Loan-to-Value Ratio (LTV) – A technical measure lenders use to assess the relationship of the loan amount to the value of the property. I.e., a borrower requesting a loan of $80,000; on a home valued at $100,000, it would have a LTV of 80 percent.

Lock In – The guarantee that the borrower will receive the rate in effect at the time of loan application.

Maintenance Fees – Payments made by the unit owner of a condominium to the homeowner's association for the expenses incurred in upkeep of the common areas.

Margin – An amount calculated in points that a lender adds to index to calculate mortgage rate adjustment.

Marketable Title – Title free of liens, clouds, and defects, a title that will be freely accepted by a buyer.

Market Value – The most likely price a given property will bring if widely exposed under normal conditions in an open market.

Mechanic's Lien – Claim placed against property by unpaid workers or suppliers.

Median Sales Price – The midpoint of the price of homes. As many homes have sold above this price as have sold below it.

Meeting of the Minds – Agreement by buyer and seller on the provisions of a contract.

Mortgage – A voluntary lien or claim against a real property given as a security to secure a loan.

Mortgage Broker – A person or company that helps borrowers find a lender. The broker doesn't make the actual loan, but receives compensation from the lender and the borrower for its services.

Mortgagee – The lender.

Mortgagor – The borrower.

Motivated Seller – A seller who has a strong desire to sell.

Mr. Nasty Pants – A term used to describe a male party to a transaction who is not very nice, likely worthy of a name far meaner. May also be used to describe a female by referring to the party as Ms. Nasty Pants. (Out of her hearing, of course.)

Multiple Listing Service (MLS) – A marketing organization comprised of member brokers who through an arrangement work together on the sale of others' listed homes, with shared and protected commissions.

Negative Amortization – Arrangement under which the shortfall in a mortgage payment is added to the amount borrowed, gradually increasing the amount of the debt.

Net listing – An arrangement under which the seller receives a specific sum from the sale price and the agent keeps the rest as sales commission. This type of listing is illegal in most states because of its vulnerability to abuses.

Offer and Acceptance – Two essential components of a valid contract; a "meeting of the minds," an agreement between the buyer and seller on the provisions of the purchase contract.

Origination Fee – An expense in obtaining a mortgage, generally for preparing and submitting a mortgage.

Personal Property – Any property that does not convey or go with the land, such as clothing, art, or furniture.

PITI – Abbreviation or acronym for principal, interest, taxes, and insurance, often lumped together in a monthly mortgage payment.

Plat – A map or chart of a lot, subdivision, or community, showing boundary lines, buildings, and easements.

PMI – Private mortgage insurance.

Point(s) – aka Discount Point(s) – The fees a lender charges a borrower when a loan is issued. One percent of a new mortgage being placed, paid in a one-time lump sum to the lender, is one point.

Portfolio Loans – Loans made by a bank or other lender that keeps its mortgages as assets in its own portfolio, rather than selling it on the secondary market.

Preapproval – The formal approval for a mortgage from the lender. To obtain this you must have submitted a standard application and had a credit check. The lender may also require proof of income, employment, and funds.

Prepayment – The payment of a mortgage loan before its due date.

Prepayment Penalty – The charge levied by the lender for paying off a mortgage before its maturity date.

Principal – (1) A sum loaned to the purchase of a home in a mortgage note. (2) The party who hires and pays the agent – generally this is the seller.

Private Mortgage Insurance (PMI) – A special type of loan insurance that many lenders require borrowers to purchase to protect the lender against default in higher LTV transactions.

Procuring Cause – Actions by a broker that bring about the desired results.

Prorations – Expenses, either prepaid or paid in arrears, that are fairly divided between buyer and seller at closing.

Purchase-Money Mortgage – A mortgage for the purchase of real property, commonly a mortgage "taken back" by the seller.

Quitclaim Deed – Deed that completely transfers whatever ownership the grantor may have had, but makes no claims of ownership in the first place.

Real Estate Owned (REO) – A property taken back through foreclosure and held for sale by a lender.

Real Property – Land and the improvements on it.

Realtor – Registered name for a member of the National Association of Realtors.

Recording – The act of entering or recording documents affecting the conveying interests in real estate in the recorder's office in the county where the property is located.

Redlining – The practice of refusing to provide loans or insurance in certain neighborhoods.

RESPA – The Real Estate Settlement Procedures Act is legislation requiring advance disclosure to the borrower of information pertinent to the loan.

Reverse Mortgage – Arrangement under which an elderly homeowner, who does not need to meet income or credit requirements, can draw against the equity in the home with no immediate repayment.

Salesperson – The holder of an entry-level license who is allowed to assist a broker who is legally responsible for the salesperson's activities

Seller's Broker – Agent who takes the seller as a client, is legally obligated to a set of fiduciary duties, and is required to put the seller's interests above all others'.

Sellers' Market – The situation in which demand for homes exceeds the supply offered for sale.

Short Sale – *A pain in the @$$.* Property sale in which the lender agrees to accept less than the mortgage amount in order to facilitate a sale and avoid a costly foreclosure.

Specific Performance – Lawsuit requiring that a contract be exactly carried out, usually asking that the seller be ordered to convey the property as previously agreed.

Slacker – A person involved in a transaction who is *not* doing what they should be doing in a timely manner to get a deal closed smoothly.

Subject To – A contingency, also a phrase often used to indicate that a buyer is not assuming mortgage liability of a seller.

Sub-agency – Legal process by which the seller who lists property for sale with a broker takes on the broker's associates and cooperating firms in a multiple listing system as agents.

Subordination Clause – A clause or provision in a mortgage document that keeps the mortgage subordinate to another mortgage; found in second mortgages.

Survey – Map made by a licensed surveyor who measures the land and charts its boundaries, improvements, and relationship to the property surrounding it.

Time is of the Essence – A legal phrase in a contract, requiring punctual performance of all obligations by all parties.

Title – (1) The rights of ownership, control, and possession of property. (2) The evidence of ownership of land such as the deed for the property.

Title Company – A company that ensures that the seller has clear, legal right to sell the property and issues a title insurance policy to protect the buyer and/or lender against possible challenges to the buyer's new title.

Title Insurance – A policy protecting the insured against loss or damage due to defects in title; the "owner's policy" protects the buyer, the "mortgagee policy" protects the lender; paid with a one time-payment at closing.

Title Search – A search of the public records, usually at the local courthouse to make sure that no adverse claims affect the value of the title.

Townhouse – An attached home that is not a condominium; the unit may share a common wall with another unit, or stand alone. Owners may also share common areas, maintained by their homeowner's association fees.

Transaction Broker – A broker who offers services without owing fiduciary duties to either party, as defined by law in various states.

Transaction Coordinator – The person who is charged with making sure that a transaction under contract gets to the closing table. Generally this is done by a highly trained administrative person; however, sometimes Realtors do this part themselves, preventing them from spending time on lead generation and follow-up or time with their family and friends.

Trust Deed – A three-party lending arrangement that includes a borrower, or trustor, an independent party stakeholder, trustee, and a lender, or beneficiary, so called because the lender stands to benefit if the trustee turns the deed over, in case the borrower fails to make payments.

VA Loan – A mortgage loan on approved property made to a qualified veteran. The Department of Veterans Affairs guarantees a veteran's mortgage so that a lender is willing to make the loan with little or no down payment.

Virtual Assistant – A skilled assistant who works remotely, generally from their home office. They do many of the things that busy professionals can't or don't have the time to do. They are often angels in disguise and have helped create many successful businesses.

Warranty Deed – The most valuable type of deed, in which the grantor makes formal assurance of the title.

Wraparound Financing – A blend of two mortgages, often used by sellers to facilitate a sale. I.e., the seller may combine the balance due on an existing mortgage with an additional loan.

Zoning – Laws of local government establishing building codes and regulations on usage of property.

"The best advice I ever got was that knowledge is power and to keep reading." David Bailey

RESOURCES

Over the years I've met some pretty spectacular people in the real estate industry and used some great products and services. I only recommend those that I have personal experience with that I know do what they say they do.

TECHIE STUFF

The inner geek in me is always looking for new things to make my life easier at work, home or on the road. Here are a few of my favorites.

TRELLO

Excellent, simple to use program for those of us who are visual to keep on top of projects and share them with our team or clients. Free and paid versions available.

www.Trello.com

GOOGLE APPS

Business level email hosting that just makes my business run smoothly. Our entire team uses this as well as the calendar integration features and contact manager. We also like to use the Google Voice feature to text with our clients. Best five dollars a month per team member I've ever spent.

www.google.com/work/apps/business/

WISE STAMP

A simple way to create powerful email signatures. Add links to your calendar, your social media and also logos or photos. Customize yours based on the different people you connect with or the businesses you run. Integrates easily with Gmail and Google Apps.

www.WiseStamp.com

EVERNOTE

I'm addicted to this one. It took me a while to get into the hang of it and now I don't know how I lived without it. For me being able to access files and notes on any devise is important. I use it for a wide variety of things including compiling research, taking notes when I'm listening to an audio program or at a seminar and also for keeping track of my favorite wines. Now when I'm at the wine store I can actually find that perfect bottle again without digging into my purse for the napkin I jotted it down on at a restaurant. Free and premium versions syncs to tablet, computer and smart phone. The possibilities are almost endless.

www.Evernote.com

EZ COORDINATOR

This is the software that my team at TMC uses to help us keep on top of all of the details from contract to close. It's robust, simple to use and cost effective.

www.EZCoordinator.com

MILE IQ

A simple little app that tracks my mileage without even having to think about it. It easily and automatically track the mileage with every car trip and gives me a handy report at the end of the year for taxes. Free and premium versions available.

www.MileIQ.com

CAMSCANNER

I use this one to turn my smart phone into a scanner. Using this app you can take a picture of a document and convert it to a PDF. Once you have it converted you can email it straight from the app. Very, very simple to use. Free version is perfect for light use or premium available if needed.

www.CamScanner.com

MARKETING AND LISTING SUPPORT SERVICES

REAL SUPOORT INC.

Located just outside Chicago, RealSupport, Inc. supports many successful real estate agents all over the country by taking over their endless marketing efforts. Time is money, and RealSupport, Inc. will save you both by assisting in all aspects of your marketing — from strategy to website design to listing coordination ,transaction management, lead management & generation, website design, logo design and more — RealSupport, Inc. fuses innovation with experience to help you succeed in a competitive market. RealSupport, Inc. is a team of experts known as Real Estate Virtual Assistants, dedicated to making you a Real Estate leader in your area. Blending creativity with technology, RealSupport, Inc. will assist you and/or your staff in whole or in part, temporarily or indefinitely.

www.RealSupportInc.com

COACHING

ANGI BELL COACHING

Angi Bell is a Results Coach who specializes in helping Real Estate professionals define a vision and set goals for their business and then craft a strategic plan to achieve those goals. She empowers her clients to overcome limiting beliefs, push beyond what they thought they could do, and embrace their greatness through bold conversations, support and accountability.

www.AngiBell.com

TRANSACTION COORDINATING

TRANSACTION MANAGEMENT CONSULTANTS

 In 2005, Michelle founded Transaction Management Consultants, LLC to help Realtors, Investors and Developers get the support they need to grow their business while providing the very best service to their buyers or sellers. Specializing only in transaction coordinating TMC has coordinated thousands and thousands of transactions for their clients all over the USA. For more information about their services visit them on the web.

www.TransactionManagementConsultants.com

WORKSHOPS AND COACHING

ENTREPRENEUR | AUTHOR | MENTOR

MICHELLE SPALDING, Coach & Mentor

For many years Michelle has been offering her services as a life and business coach to entrepreneurs. For more information on her coaching programs or to attend one of her workshops go to www.MichelleSpalding.com

TRANSACTION COORDINATOR TRAINING

When you know you're called to be in the real estate industry, but aren't sue that sales is your thing, being a transaction coordinator may be your true calling. If you're not sure how to start your career as a TC or already have and are ready to make your career a business or are just looking for support to help you in your TC business, the TCA is the place for you. Check out the course offerings and programs available exclusively for TCs at www.TransactionCoordinatorAcademy.com

FORMS AND SAMPLE DOCS

Throughout the book I referenced several forms and guides that are available on my website. You can pick up a copy in Word format for additional editing and use in your real estate business at www.ContractToCloseForms.com

ABOUT THE AUTHOR

Michelle Spalding is a passionate entrepreneur who loves life and lives with her family in the Western Suburbs of Chicago. She's a licensed real estate broker in Florida. In 2005, she founded Transaction Management Consultants, LLC to help her fellow real estate agents get the leverage they needed to continue to grow their real estate business. In 2015, she founded the Transaction Coordinators Academy, an organization dedicated to ensuring the professionalism of real estate transaction coordinators nationwide.

Several years ago she discovered she has a real passion and gift for coaching other entrepreneurs and helping them to create the life and business they desire. She is often ask to speak at real estate events and small business events where she shares her enthusiasm and experience in creating a business that allows her to focus on her gifts and talents while having a team help her with all of the other details necessary. When she's not busy with her work she's you'll find her playing with her granddaughter, traveling, attending music concerts, sipping wine or curled up on the sofa reading a book with her cat Pia.

Michelle is all over the web. You can get social with her at:

www.linkedin.com/in/michellespalding
twitter.com/mdspalding

https://www.instagram.com/michellespalding
www.facebook.com/TransactionManagementConsultants
www.facebook.com/TransactionCoordinatorAcademy

Check out her websites here:

www.MichelleSpalding.com
www.TransactionManagementConsultants.com
www.TransactionCoordinatorsAcademy.com

Feel free to send gifts and letters here:

Michelle Spalding
P.O. Box 4225
St. Charles, IL 60174